THE
TWELFTH
INSIGHT

Also by James Redfield

The Celestine Prophecy
The Celestine Prophecy: An Experiential Guide (with Carol Adrienne)
The Tenth Insight: Holding the Vision
The Tenth Insight: An Experiential Guide (with Carol Adrienne)
The Celestine Vision: Living the New Spiritual Awareness
The Secret of Shambhala: In Search of the Eleventh Insight
God and the Evolving Universe: The Next Step in Personal Evolution
(with Sylvia Timbers and Michael Murphy)

THE TWELFTH INSIGHT

The Hour of Decision

JAMES REDFIELD

GRAND CENTRAL
PUBLISHING

NEW YORK   BOSTON

Grand Central Publishing
Hachette Book Group
237 Park Avenue
New York, NY 10017

www.HachetteBookGroup.com

Printed in the United States of America

First Edition: February 2011

10 9 8 7 6 5 4 3 2 1

Grand Central Publishing is a division of Hachette Book Group, Inc.
The Grand Central Publishing name and logo is a trademark of Hachette Book Group, Inc.

The publisher is not responsible for websites (or their content) that are not owned by the publisher.

Library of Congress Cataloging-in-Publication Data

Redfield, James.
    The twelfth insight : the hour of decision / James Redfield. — 1st ed.
        p. cm.
    Summary: "The fourth book in the Celestine Series, this is an adventure tale, both suspenseful and contemplative, that describes a new wave of religious tolerance and integrity that is arriving, in reaction to years of religious warfare and political corruption"—Provided by publisher.
    ISBN 978-0-446-57596-6
    1. Religious tolerance—Fiction. 2. Spiritual life—Fiction. I. Title.
    PS3568.E3448T84 2011
    813'.54—dc22   2010046509

For Kaelynn and Mckenna

ACKNOWLEDGMENTS

I'm in gratitude for many people who in some way contributed to this book. First and foremost, I would like to thank the many individuals worldwide, existing across all religions, who keep the idea of an authentic spiritual consciousness alive and thriving. It is your quiet fortitude that is literally saving the day.

Also, special mention goes to Larry Dossey for his book *The Power of Premonitions*. He somehow always produces a landmark work just when it is time to popularize a step forward in human awareness. Thanks to Dr. Russell Blaylock, who leads the fight against dangerous chemical additives in our food. And Michael Murphy, who holds the space for so many who seek to bridge the great human divides of our time: first the Cold War, and now Religious and Cultural Intolerance. Also I'd like to acknowledge the work of Carl Johan Calleman and John Major Jenkins concerning the Mayan Calendar. And a sincere thanks goes to Phil Cousineau for his brilliant analysis of comparative religious thought.

Closer to home, I must say many thanks to Larry Kirshbaum, and my publisher Jamie Raab, who grasped the vision and helped to shape its ideas; to the many people at Grand Central Publishing who help turn a manuscript into a book; to Kelly Leavitt, whose artful eye always tracks for impact and comprehension; to Albert Clayton Gaulden, for his cosmological timing; and to Larry Miller, whose many conversations have sparked my thinking. Also, thanks to Steve Maraboli, whose Better Today community is a prime example of the emerging Twelfth Insight.

Most of all, I'd like to express gratitude and love to my wife, Salle, whose support and deep insight nurtured my spirit along the way.

CONTENTS

Sustaining Synchronicity   *1*

Conscious Conversation   *19*

Moving into Alignment   *43*

Recognizing Ideology   *65*

The God Connection   *84*

The Great Commissioning   *100*

The Art of Tuning In   *121*

The Oneness Intention   *137*

Opening to Perception   *156*

What Heaven Knows   *174*

The Rise to Influence   *193*

The Return   *210*

Epilogue   *224*

THE
TWELFTH
INSIGHT

In a time of universal deceit, truth-telling
becomes a revolutionary act.

—GEORGE ORWELL

SUSTAINING SYNCHRONICITY

I turned onto the freeway and hit cruise control, trying to ease up a bit. There was plenty of time to meet Wil at the airport. So I forced myself to relax and take in the autumn sunshine and the rolling southern hills. Not to mention the flocks of crows slinking along the shoulders of the highway.

The crows, I knew, were a good sign, even if I had been battling with them all summer. In folklore, their presence indicates mystery and an impending rendezvous with one's own destiny. Some say they will even lead you to such a moment, if you chance to follow them long enough.

Unfortunately, they will also show up in the early mornings to eat the young pea plants in your backyard garden—unless, of course, you make a deal. They laugh at scarecrows and shotguns. But if you give them their own row of plants near the forest, they will tend to leave the rest alone.

Just then, a single crow flew over the car and out in front of me. Then turned completely around and headed back the way I'd come. I tried to follow it in the rearview mirror, but all I could see was a dark blue SUV about a hundred yards back.

Thinking nothing of the vehicle, I continued to watch the

scenery, taking in a deep breath and hitting another level of relaxation. A road trip, I thought, nothing like it. I wondered how many people, in how many places, were experiencing this exact kind of moment—getting away from the stress of an unsure world, just to see what might happen.

Only, in my case, I was also looking for something. For months now, I had been running into total strangers all talking about the same thing: the secret release of an old, unnamed Document. Supposedly, it had come from a coalition representing the world's religious traditions, and word of it was already widespread, at least among those with an ear for such things. Yet no one seemed to have any details. Rumor had it that it was now being released ahead of schedule, out of necessity.

For me, the rumors were both intriguing and slightly humorous. The idea of a coalition among the religious traditions was hardly new, but it had always proven to be all but impossible in reality. The differences in beliefs were just too great. And in the end, each tradition wanted to prevail over the others.

In fact, I had been ready to dismiss the rumors when something else had occurred: I received a fax from Wil. He sent me two translated pages, ostensibly from this old Document. In the margin of the first page was a notation in Wil's handwriting saying, "This has both Hebrew and Arabic origins."

As I read the pages, it seemed to be a treatment of modern times, proclaiming that something important was going to begin in the second decade of the twenty-first century. I grimaced at the date, thinking it might be one more end-of-the-world prophecy—another in a long line of doomsday predictions misinterpreting everything from the Mayan Calendar to Nostradamus to Revelation. All shouting to the ends of the Earth: "Haven't you heard, the world is ending in 2012!"

For years now, the media had been pushing the "end times"

scenario, and people, though worried, also seemed deeply intrigued. The big question was why? What could be causing this fascination? Is it just the excitement over being alive at the precise time the Mayan Calendar is scheduled to end? Or was it something else? Maybe, just maybe, our fascination with the end revealed a latent intuition, increasingly noticeable, that something better was about to be born.

The more I read of Wil's fax, the more the pages began to carry a kind of numinous attraction. The style was upbeat and vaguely familiar in some way, and the authentic tone was confirmed when I saw a second notation from Wil on the last page. "This came from a friend," he had scribbled. "It's for real."

I looked over at the very same fax pages lying on the passenger seat beside me. Light from the afternoon sun flickered over them. Wil's written comment, I knew, meant that the original was, at least in his mind, well founded—and probably extended the message of what had always been his singular obsession: the old Celestine Prophecy that had been discovered in Peru.

The thought spawned a flood of memories as I recalled how quickly word of the First Nine Insights of this Prophecy had circulated around the planet. Why? Because they made sense in a world too shallow and materialistic. The message of this Prophecy was clear. Being spiritual is more than merely believing in some deity in the abstract. It entails the discovery of another, entirely different dimension of life, one that operates solely in a spiritual manner.

Once one makes this discovery, one realizes the universe is filled with all sorts of fortuitous encounters, intuitions, and mysterious coincidences, all pointing to a higher purpose behind our lives, and in fact, behind all of human history. The only question, then, for the seeker who wakes up to this reality is how does this mysterious world really operate, and how does one begin to engage its secrets.

In those days, I knew, something had popped in human consciousness and had led directly to two more Insights: a Tenth and Eleventh. The Tenth delved into the mystery of the Afterlife and chronicled a decadelong focus on Heaven and its inhabitants, forever dispelling, along the way, an age-old repression of death and what happens afterward. Once that block was lifted, an exploration of everything spiritual seemed to begin.

Quickly came the next Insight: the Eleventh, born of a collective knowing that we are all here to participate in some as yet undefined agenda—a Plan of some kind. It involved the discovery of how to manifest our deepest dreams and to lift the world to its ideal. In the years that followed, this intuition grew into all sorts of theories about Secrets and Prayer Power and Laws of Attraction, theories that seemed right but not quite complete.

Those theories, I knew, brought us up to recent times and lasted until the material bottom fell out from under all of us—in the form of a worldwide financial collapse. After that, we faced more immediate matters, such as personal solvency and not letting the doomsayers take us too far into fear. We were still awake, and we still wanted more spiritual answers. But from then on, those answers had to be practical as well. They had to work in the real world, no matter how mysterious that world turned out to be.

I felt a smile coming up....How interesting that Wil had found these writings now. He had long predicted the emergence of another Insight, the Twelfth—which he felt would signal a final revelation for humanity, picking up where the Eleventh had left off. I wondered, would the Twelfth finally show us how to "live" this spiritual knowledge at a greater level? Would this change begin to usher in this new, more ideal world we seemed to sense was coming?

I knew we would have to wait and see. Wil had said only to meet him at the airport and from there we would head to Cairo, if it worked out. If it worked out? What did he mean by that?

*   *   *

A deer dashing across the freeway broke my rumination, and I tapped the brakes to slow down. The big doe ran full speed across six lanes and jumped the fence on the other side. A deer was also a good sign, a symbol of attention and alertness.

As I looked out at the hills then, their fall colors now bathed in the light of an amber-tinted sunset, I realized I felt exactly that way: more alert and alive. All these thoughts had somehow induced a greater energy level in me, lifting me to a place where I was attending to every detail—the sunset, the landscape whizzing by, the thoughts entering my mind—as though everything was suddenly more important somehow.

Another huge smile spontaneously erupted. This was a state of mind I'd experienced many times before. And every time it happened, it caught me totally by surprise—surprise in one way over its sudden occurrence, and in another way over why I had ever lost it in the first place, it seemed so right and natural.

There were many names for this experience—the Zone, Heightened Perception, and my favorite, Synchronistic Flow—all names seeking to capture its central characteristic: a sudden elevation in one's experience, wherein we transcend the ordinary and find a higher meaning in the flow of events. This Synchronistic perception "centers" us in some way and feels beyond what could be expected from pure chance—as though a higher "destiny" is unfolding.

Suddenly, a building coming up on the right caught my eye. It was a little sports bar called the Pub that Wil had pointed out years ago as having good eats and homemade pies. I had passed it many times but had never stopped. Plenty of time now, I thought. Why not grab a bite here and avoid the airport food? I took the exit and headed down the ramp. The SUV behind me also took the turn.

*   *   *

After parking under a gigantic oak tree in the fading light, I walked inside, finding the place full of people. Couples talked around the bar, and families with kids ate casually at six or seven tables in the middle of the room. My eyes immediately fixed on two women sitting at a table against the far wall. They were leaning toward each other and talking intensely. As I made my way in that direction, I noticed a small table open beside them.

When I sat down, the younger of the two women glanced at me for a moment and then turned back to her friend.

"The First Integration," she said, "suggests there's a way to keep the Synchronicity going. But I don't have all of the Document. More of these writings exist somewhere. I have to find them."

My energy surged again. Was she talking about the same Document? The woman speaking was wearing jeans and comfortable hiking shoes, and around her neck was draped a multicolored scarf. As she spoke, she kept pushing her blonde, tapered bangs behind her ears. I caught the faint scent of rose perfume.

As I watched her, I felt an odd attraction, which shocked me. She looked around instinctively and caught me staring, making deep eye contact. I quickly turned away. When I glanced back, a short, stocky man walked up to her table, surprising the two women and creating a round of smiles and hugs. The woman with the scarf gave him several typed pages, which he silently read. I pretended to look over the menu as I waited, sensing all the more that something important was happening.

"Why are you going to Arizona?" the man asked.

"Because it keeps coming to mind, over and over again," she replied. "I have to go with it."

I listened intently. All of the people at the table seemed to be at the same level of flow that I was.

"I have to understand why my mother contacted me," the woman continued. "These writings are going to tell me. I know it."

"So you're leaving right away?" the man asked.

"Yes, tonight," she replied.

"Just follow your intuition," the man interjected. "Synchronicity seems to be happening for you. But be careful. Who knows who's looking for this information?"

I couldn't stand it any longer. I was about to say something to them when a large, muscular man at a table near mine mumbled, "What a crock!"

"W-w-what?" I stammered.

He nodded toward the women and whispered, "What they're saying. What a bunch of bull!"

For a moment, I didn't know how to respond. He was tall and about forty-five, with unruly brown hair and a frown on his face, leaning toward me in his chair.

He shook his head. "This is going to be the death of our civilization, this kind of magical thinking."

Jeez, I thought, a skeptic. I didn't have time for this.

He was reading my face. "What? You agree with them?"

I just looked away, trying to hear what the woman was saying, but he scooted his chair closer.

"Intuition is a myth!" he said firmly. "It's been disproved many times. Thoughts are just nerve firings in the brain reflecting whatever you think you know about your environment. And Doctor Jung's crap about Synchronicity is just the act of seeing what you want to see in the random events of the world. I know. I'm a scientist."

He grinned slightly, seemingly pleased that he knew the origin of the theory of Synchronicity. I, on the other hand, was getting more irritated.

"Look," I said, "I'd rather not talk about it."

I turned to listen again but it was too late. The woman and her friends were up and walking toward the door. The skeptic gave me a smirk and then got up and walked out as well. I thought about following them but decided against it, concerned I'd look like a stalker or something. I sat back down. The moment had been lost.

As I sat there, I knew the energy I had marshaled in the car had totally vanished. I now felt flat and uninspired. I even pondered, fleetingly, whether the skeptic might be correct in his assessment, but quickly shook off the idea. Too much had occurred in my life for me to believe that now. More likely, what I thought had happened, had happened. I was on the verge of finding out more about the Document when I was bushwhacked by the bane of my life: a skeptic out to debunk everything spiritual.

I might have gone on in my funk had I not suddenly noticed an individual staring at me from the corner of the room near the door. He was dressed in a brown leather jacket and had short hair. A pair of sunglasses hung from his shirt pocket. When our eyes met, he stepped behind a group of people bunched up at the bar.

Carefully, I looked around the room and caught two more people looking at me, all dressed in varying casual attire but sporting the same monotonal stare. They also looked away when I saw them.

Great, I thought. These were professional operatives of some kind. I got up and eased toward the restroom. None of them reacted. Walking past it down a small hallway, I found what I was hoping for, a back door. I walked out to the poorly lit parking lot, seeing no one. Then, as I got closer to my vehicle, a figure ducked behind a panel truck. When I started walking again, the person began to walk as well, angling to cut me off.

I stopped and he stopped, and then I saw something familiar in his posture. It was Wil! When I got to him, he pulled me down and looked back at the Pub.

"What are you into here, my friend?" he asked in his customary half-humorous tone.

"I don't know," I blurted. "I saw several people watching me inside. What are you doing here, Wil?"

I noticed for the first time that he was carrying a large trekking backpack.

He nodded toward my vehicle. "I'll tell you later. That's your Cruiser, right? Let's get out of here. I'll drive."

As we entered the automobile, I looked over at the far end of the parking lot and spotted the woman with the scarf standing with several others. Shockingly, one was the skeptic.

I wanted to continue watching, but I saw something beyond them that startled me even more. The blue SUV I had noticed behind me earlier was parked a hundred feet away, near a back fence. Even at this distance, I could see two men sitting in the front seats.

I grimaced. I should have known.

As I watched behind us, Wil drove us to the freeway and turned north. No one seemed to be following.

"Why did you come here to the Pub?" I asked again.

"Just a hunch," he said. "I didn't know how else I could find you. I began to see people watching me, too, so I didn't want to use a cell. A friend was driving me to the airport, and I remembered this place and thought you might have stopped. When we found your car, I had him drop me off."

He looked closely at me. "What about you? Why did you decide to stop here?"

"I saw the Pub from the freeway and remembered you pointing it out. I thought it would be a good place to grab some food...."

He smiled at me knowingly. We both knew it was pure Synchronicity. As I looked at him, I noticed that he had aged well in the past few years since I had seen him. There were more lines in his tanned face, but his movements and voice made him seem like a man much younger. His eyes still sparkled with alertness.

"There are more people looking for this document than I thought," he mused. "Better tell me everything that's happened to you."

As we traveled north, I relayed all of it: the ideas that came to me while driving, the blue SUV, the sudden flow of Synchronicity, and every detail of what I'd experienced at the pub—especially the part where the skeptic brought me down and the men were observing me.

When I finished, I didn't wait for him to comment. I asked him about the surveillance.

"I don't know who they are," he said. "I started to have the feeling I was being observed a few days ago. Then yesterday, I saw one or two of them at a distance. They're very good."

I nodded, feeling nervous. I lifted the pages of translation by my leg and asked, "Who sent this to you?"

"A friend who lives in Egypt," Wil replied, "one of the foremost experts in ancient texts. I've known him a long time, and when we talked by phone he said it's unquestionably authentic and probably dates back to the fourth or fifth century. He was sent only the first part of the Document, already translated, but he thinks it refers to our current time period, just like the old Prophecy did."

We exchanged glances.

"There's more," Wil continued. "The Document says we're in some kind of a race here. My friend said these fragments are popping up all over the world. Apparently, whoever is releasing this Document is sending selected parts to various people with some end in mind. That's all I know. My friend and I were disconnected in the middle of the call. I haven't been able to reach him since."

My mind was abuzz. The woman I saw at the Pub had a part

of the Document and was going to Arizona. But where in Arizona? Was she in danger? Were we?

The reality of the situation was sinking in. The Document was fascinating, but we had just seen that someone official also had an interest as well. Were they trying to restrict access to it? How far would they go? A pang of fear rushed through me.

"Well, I guess our trip to Egypt is off," I said, looking for humor.

Wil grinned for a moment. "I had a feeling we might be going somewhere else."

Suddenly, he looked hard into the rearview mirror. Behind us was another SUV, a long way back.

"I think this one's following us," he said.

At this point Wil began a series of strategic moves. First, he asked to borrow my smart phone and pulled up the map of the local area, turned the phone off, and pulled out the battery. Then he slowed down, which made the SUV slow down as well in order to keep its distance behind us. After a minute, Will quickly sped up, a move that opened a lot more space between us and the SUV and allowed Wil to take the next exit unseen.

He took an immediate right onto a small paved road, then a left onto a gravel road that I knew wouldn't have been on the map.

"How did you know about this road?" I asked.

He shot me a look but said nothing. The old road was full of potholes and ruts, but it eventually led to another paved road that in turn took us back to the freeway again, about five miles farther north. When we hit the ramp it became clear that the freeway behind us was completely backed up. We could see blue lights and a fire truck parked at the point of congestion.

Wil sped down the ramp and onto what was an almost empty road. Everyone else behind us, including those in the SUV, was completely blocked.

I was staring at Wil. In the past I had seen him do many things, but nothing this rapid.

"How did you know to make all those turns?" I asked.

He looked at me and asked in return, "How did you know to stop at the Pub so that we could connect with each other later?"

"Okay," I acknowledged. "Intuition. But what you did seemed so fast. I've never done anything like that."

Light from the oncoming cars swept over his face. "I've been talking to people who have seen different parts of this Document. It describes many abilities humans haven't developed yet. That's what this Document seems to be all about. Each part is devoted to what it calls the 'Integration' of spiritual knowledge, and it refers directly to the insights of the old Prophecy."

"Wait a minute," I said. "That would mean the author of this Document, whoever it was, had to have known about the Prophecy, way back then."

"Yeah." I think it's some kind of companion piece, like a guide. My friend said there are eleven parts of this Document floating around out there, each devoted to a particular Integration of knowledge. And it talks about a Twelfth...."

"It reveals what the Twelfth Insight is?" I asked.

"Apparently, but no one seems to have that part yet, or at least no one is talking about it. The Document says that each Integration must be actualizd in order, one after the other, beginning with the First: learning to sustain Synchronicity."

He paused and looked at me, adding, "That has always been a problem."

I knew what he was getting at. Everyone glimpses Synchronicity. The challenge, just as in my case, was to sustain the experience and keep the flow going. Of all the difficulties with Synchronicity, this was the one most people voiced. Synchronistic experience seemed to come into our lives almost as a tease, stay a while, and then end.

Turning around, I gazed behind us again to check the road, finding it still clear. I remained nervous.

"I'm not sure I want to get involved with this Document, Wil. It may be too dangerous."

He nodded. "What do you want to do?"

"I want to go to a police station and get these people off of us. Maybe I can help get the word out after the contents are known."

"What if that doesn't happen? And the Twelfth is never found?"

I looked at him and smiled. We'd been though a lot in the past, and Wil had never steered me wrong. I wanted to hear what he had to say.

"Look," he continued. "All that we've discovered, the whole search for the truth about spiritual experience, it may be coming down to this moment. You decide, but at least let me tell you what's at stake."

Wil slowed the car and exited the freeway, saying he wanted to concentrate. He noticed a little side road just off the ramp and backed in and turned the lights off.

"The Document speaks very directly," he began. "It says that during the current period of history, the easy material life will get harder, with widespread financial and social disruption. Yet it proclaims that all the challenges are evoking an even greater spiritual awakening in us, where we can realize many new abilities and perceptions.

"But each of us has to make a decision. Will we embrace this deeper spirituality, or go into fear and foreboding? It is a challenge of courage, but also of practicality. In some sense, events are forcing us to put our beliefs into action. The only way to survive the level of turmoil we are facing in the world is to pursue life in a different way.

"It says the first ability that will manifest is our being able to sustain Synchronistic Flow. When the mysterious coincidences come more frequently, we'll eventually learn that we are guided, even protected, from the dangers of this historical period."

He paused and caught my eye in the dim light. "There's more. The Document says that those of us, early on, who discover how to sustain this flow and integrate this knowledge will make it easier for others to open up to it later, just because of the influence we have.

"But on the other hand, if too many of us fail to move forward in this regard, the knowledge might not be actualized at all and could be lost to history."

"It says that?"

"Yes, exactly that."

He smiled at me in a sympathetic way.

"That's how important it is," he continued. "Yet we all have to make our own individual choices."

"Tell me more."

"The Document focuses on the Synchronistic experience first," Wil continued, "because it is the phenomenon that leads each of us forward. If we make this experience more consistent, then we realize our lives are trying to take off in a destined direction. We feel more alive."

Exactly, I thought. More alive. I'd used that exact expression earlier to describe my own experience. And because I had just been thinking of the release of the Document, I knew the meeting was beyond chance when I saw the women and heard their conversation. I was meant to be there somehow. Then, of course, the skeptic appeared and the experience was lost. I could feel my energy drop even now, just thinking about it.

Wil seemed to notice. "When we enter a flow of Synchronicity, clarity and aliveness is what we get. When we fall out of the flow, it is what we lose.

"The point is, we have the opportunity now to finally reach a higher clarity about not just the phenomenon of Synchronicity, but also about our entire spiritual nature. And if we don't, then all our futures, and the futures of our children, could go in an entirely different direction."

He paused as a car moved along the road in front of us. It passed us and seemed to be of no concern.

"So the idea is this: we find the pieces of this Document, one at a time. Each part builds upon the previous one, so they integrate seamlessly together, yielding both a greater understanding and a higher consciousness, and all these new abilities.

"The Document says when we integrate all eleven, we get the final download: the Twelfth. After that, we'll understand not just the full picture of spirituality in this life, but we'll be able live it most of the time."

Another car went by.

"But again," Wil continued, "the First Integration gets the whole thing going, because it involves learning how to stay in the flow of Synchronicity that will lead us forward."

"What does it say about staying in Synchronistic Flow?" I asked.

"It says all we have to do is learn to remember."

"Remember what?"

"That this flow is possible! That it exists! In the past, when you first read the Insights of the Prophecy, and we were all thinking and talking about Synchronicity, didn't it seem to happen a lot?

Well, that was literally because we had the expectation of it in mind. That's all it takes. All you have to do is remember to remember."

I had to think about this for a moment. Was it that simple? Earlier, as I was driving to the Pub, I certainly let go and began thinking about the reality of Synchronicity. And yes, I suddenly fell right into it.

"In practice," Wil clarified, "it boils down to consciously expecting the next Synchronicity to come, which means we should go into a posture of 'expectant alertness,' a mood that's not that easy right now, because we always think we're behind, with too much to do. But staying in this state of alertness helps us immediately, because it has the effect of 'slowing down' time."

I knew that was exactly true. Anytime you are expecting something and want it to hurry up and happen, it takes forever to arrive. Time does seem to slow down.

"Slowing down time is a good thing right now," he added, "because so many of us feel overwhelmed by problems coming at us at light speed. The more we can slow everything down—and wait on a Synchronistic event to show us the way—the easier life is to handle.

"So, to begin, we have to put a sticky note on the bathroom mirror, or tell a friend to call us first thing in the morning, anything to remind ourselves to set up an expectation for Synchronicity first thing each day. Eventually, it becomes a habit. And once all the mysterious coincidences are happening and our destiny seems to be unfolding, all that is left is to stay in that flow."

He paused dramatically.

"And to do that," he went on, "we have to learn to communicate what's going on with us to others."

"What?"

"Think about what happens when we lose the Flow," he explained. "Doesn't it occur because we hit some situation where we have to interact with others who aren't in a flow, and who can't readily see the meanings we are seeing? The effect is to knock us out of it altogether."

I thought about what happened to me with the skeptic. It was certainly true in that case.

"When I'm in the flow," I said, "I usually try to get away from most people, so they can't knock me out of it."

"I know," Wil said in a mock accusatory tone.

"Are you saying," I asked, "that I should have taken the time to talk with that skeptic, even though that's not what I wanted to do?"

"No, I'm suggesting that you should have been open and truthful with him, maybe asking him to wait a minute while you talked to the people at the table. He was needling you, but you didn't lose your flow because of him. You lost it because you didn't find a way to honestly communicate who you were and what you were doing."

"I don't think he was interested in hearing anything from me."

"You're missing the point. I'm not telling you to defend yourself or to convince him of anything. You just have to give him the truth of the situation as you see it, with the main purpose being to keep yourself centered in the flow. If he'd walked away or thought you were rude, so be it, but you would have held your flow."

Again he paused dramatically, then said, "And by handling it that way, you would have also stayed open to whether he had some information for *you*! You know from the old Prophecy in Peru that you must treat his perceived interruption not as a threat but as a potential Synchronicity itself—in the long run, perhaps being of equal importance to what you were learning from the woman."

The reminder both jolted and invigorated me at the same time. If I was getting all this right, then telling the truth of one's situation, whatever it happened to be, kept the flow going—and primarily because it kept one centered in the clarity of one's own deeper life experience. Again, I had to question whether it could be this simple.

When I voiced the question to Wil, he chuckled and said, "It's as simple and as hard as that. And if you want to follow through with finding the Integrations, you have to start by concentrating on telling the absolute truth, to yourself and others, about what is happening to you—no matter how esoteric it gets."

As I continued to think, Wil started the car and pulled onto the freeway again. After a short distance, he moved into the left lane to avoid a car parked on the right shoulder. Inside was the silhouette of a lone driver. Light flickered across his face.

"That's him!" I stammered, not quite believing it. "The skeptic at the Pub. That's him."

Wil looked back. "Are you sure?"

"Yes."

As we watched, the man pulled onto the freeway and took the first exit he came to. Wil glanced questioningly at me.

"What?" I asked.

"You look like you're more in the flow now. Perhaps you're being given another chance."

"You mean to talk with him?"

"Well," Wil said, looking at the dash, "you wanted to know where the woman you saw was going. And you said he was talking to her in the parking lot. We need gas, so we could go back and find him."

I looked at Wil and nodded, not exactly liking it. "Okay, I'm in. But I'm not sure I'll know what to say to this guy."

"Just tell him the truth," Wil said, "that you believe meaningful coincidences are real, and occur for a reason...and this is the second time you've crossed paths with him."

CONSCIOUS CONVERSATION

We turned around and took the same exit and pulled up to a huge, well-lit truck stop. A dozen trucks were lined up behind a main building that housed a restaurant, showers, and store. Only a few cars were at the gasoline pumps. The skeptic's brown rental was one of them.

"Remember," Wil offered, "carry the attitude of expecting Synchronicity all the way into the conversation. I like the movie analogy. Synchronistic Flow feels as though you are slowing down and increasing your feeling that you are the center, or star, of your own unfolding movie. Keep this centered clarity and you'll know what to say."

Wil smiled and pulled the Cruiser up to a pump directly across from the skeptic, then made one more comment.

"The Document says," he added, "that if you commit to holding your truth, it includes all the ideas that come up intuitively to say to him, even if you've never thought of the ideas before."

I nodded and got out and began putting gas in the Cruiser, feeling that numinous sensation again, as though this was going to be an immensely important conversation for everything that was going to happen later.

The skeptic was directly across from me, busy fueling his own vehicle. Finally, he spotted me and laughed out loud.

"Well, it's the lover of coincidences," he said. "What a Synchronicity this is!"

"Maybe," I said. "We passed you back on the freeway, and we turned around to talk to you."

I couldn't quite believe that I had started off that directly, but it did seem to help me stay centered.

"And what do you think we have to talk about?" he asked.

His tone was sarcastic, yet semifriendly, and I suddenly realized he was speaking in the jousting style favored by scientists, a mode of talking that is more like a friendly debate. The key element of this style is to take great care not to inadvertently confirm some idea or theory held by the other party. In the world of Science, to affirm a colleague's position is never something to be taken lightly. It has to be earned. So the idea is to be very skeptical at first and to check out whether the person is carrying the proper scientific attitude.

If the other party crosses the line and takes a position that is poorly thought out or too speculative, then the conversation is over immediately. On the other hand, if the other person is being logical and tentative with his pronouncements, then the debate can go on. I had always thought communicating in this manner was boring and time consuming, but I knew I could do it.

"I don't know," I replied, "whether we have anything to talk about or not. I guess we'll have to see. I'm trying to make contact with the woman we saw back at the Pub. She was talking about an old Document, and I noticed you speaking with her outside, later. Did she tell you where in Arizona she was going?"

"What's your interest in this document?" he asked guardedly.

"I'm interested in what it says about spirituality."

He looked at me sharply. "You think it's going to confirm your ideas about Synchronicity?"

"The part we have has already done that."

He shook his head. "I wouldn't give this kind of writing too much weight. The best it could do is add to our knowledge of some ancient people's mythology and superstition."

"Yeah, but you can compare what it says to your own experience and go from there."

"In order to do what?"

"To identify phenomena to be investigated that may have been missed before."

He gazed at me questioningly.

"Look," I said, "I believe that there's more to the Universe than a strictly skeptical attitude allows into experience. Sometimes you have to bracket your skepticism long enough to fully experience a new phenomenon. Don't you ever wonder if there is something real and universal behind people's spiritual experiences?"

He gave me a hint of a smile. I wasn't convincing him, but I could tell he liked my tact.

"We need Science," I added. "But we need it to look at everything."

"What do you know of Science?" he asked, giving me a superior look. "Science is a very precise process where individuals explore and draw conclusions about the nature of the world around them. And its activity is very precise: one scientist suggests that something in nature works a certain way, and other scientists try to refute that hypothesis with other facts they think are true. Slowly, consensus is reached about the issue. In turn, this conclusion about reality is replaced with something that is even more true, and so on. That's how scientific fact, and the resulting social reality that flows from it, is established. It's a precise, orderly process."

He looked away and added, "At least that's the way it's supposed to work."

"What do you mean?" I asked.

"Well, lately a lot of corruption has happened: moneyed interests such as big pharmaceutical companies and food processors
have taken over the medical schools and university departments
with big grants, and now they get the results they want from studies. Other industries do the same thing, but health and food are the
worst. It's pitiful."

I thought of the writings of Dr. Russell Blaylock, who talks about
why dangerous additives still remain in our food, then realized
something in a flash: this skeptic I'm talking to is an idealist.

Something else came into my mind to say, and I recalled Wil
stressing that such ideas had to be voiced.

"Look," I stated, "maybe the key is heightening public awareness of the scientific process, and then applying it to every part of
our world. What if this document is right about Synchronicity being
a part of the natural order of things? Shouldn't it be investigated
with the same vigor as a star or bacteria?"

Something about what I said irritated him, and he took the gas
nozzle out of his car and slammed it back in its place at the pump.

"W-w-what I'm saying," he stammered, "is that something like
this document can't be trusted. Synchronicity is too subjective. The
problem with Science now is that the emphasis on basic truth is
being lost. Once we start allowing too much speculation or corruption, the culture can slip into fantasy thinking and even delusionary
movements."

He was looking at me hard. "Don't you see that civilization is
hanging by a thread? It only takes so many people losing a grip on
the basic laws of nature to undermine logical thinking and scientifi-
cally established reality altogether. And if that happens we fall back
into superstition and a new dark age."

I nodded and said, "But what if a science of spirituality could be
logical and orderly?"

He didn't answer. Instead he shook his head and walked into

the building to pay. Wil was still seated behind the wheel and smiling at me. He had heard the entire conversation through the open car window.

"Aren't you going to get into this?" I asked.

"Nope," he said. "I think it's yours to finish."

When the scientist came out of the building, I approached him again.

"Look," I said, "you're right. No one wants a new dark age. But let me pose the issue in another way: what would it take for scientists like you to be able to study spiritual phenomena in a way that *is* orderly and logical?"

For a long moment he seemed to be genuinely considering my question. "I don't know.... We would have to discover something like the natural laws of spirituality—"

He stopped and shook his head, then waved me off.

"Listen," he said. "I really don't have time for any more speculation. Believe me, none of this is going to happen."

I nodded and then introduced myself. He shook my hand and said his name was Dr. John Coleman.

"Enjoyed the conversation," I said. "Maybe I'll see you another time."

He chuckled at that and then said, "The woman you were asking about... her name is Rachel Banks. She was going to a town north of Phoenix, a little place called Sedona."

I sat up straight in the passenger seat, struggling to wake up. As we drove along, sunlight from behind us was just beginning to fill the car, and the sweet smell of Oklahoma farmland filled my nostrils. Wil nodded when he saw me stirring, then immediately looked back at the road, appearing to be deep in thought.

Which was fine with me; I was talked out. Because we both knew Sedona well, Wil and I had conversed late into the night as we traveled west. For years, the town had been a hotbed of spiritual thought, as it was situated in the famous red rock hills of Native American lore. Because the energy was so strong there, it was claimed by some that the town had more houses of worship, new age centers, and artists per square mile than any place in America.

The question that had most intrigued us last night concerned Rachel's motivations. Why were her intuitions pointing to Sedona? Was it because one would likely find more people talking about such writings there? Or was it because one could understand esoteric information in general at a deeper level just by being in those hills—the famous "Sedona effect"?

I shook off the thoughts. All I wanted to do at this point was look out at the landscape. We had traveled from the mountains of Georgia and Tennessee to the flatlands of Oklahoma, and now the sky was big and blue in the morning light. Munching on nuts and apples that Wil had packed for breakfast, I watched the scenery go by for a while.

When I awakened fully, I noticed two neat stacks of pages on top of the dashboard in front of me. I looked over at Wil, figuring he had placed the stacks in front of me for a reason. He kept his eyes on the road but lifted one eyebrow, which made me chuckle. I reached over, grabbed the stack on the left, and began to read.

The pages described the First Integration almost exactly as Wil had relayed it earlier, and then reiterated that once Synchronicity was being sustained, one should be on high alert—for it was that mysterious flow that would reveal the other Integrations.

Reading on, the Document divided the twelve total Integrations into two groups. It called the first five Integrations the "Foundation" of spiritual consciousness, and the remainder it called the "Rise to Sacred Influence."

Rise to Influence? I had no idea what that meant, but I remembered that Wil had said those of us pursuing the Integrations now would make it easier for others to do so later because of some kind of mysterious influence.

Coming to the end of the first stack, I picked up the other stack of text, which began to address the Second Integration. This step up in consciousness begins, it said, when we realize that human conversation, regardless of the subject, is always an exchange of outlook, or worldview—and thus is the basic mechanism of human evolution, taking us from one historical level of knowledge to the next.

When human interaction is done while in centered, Synchronistic truth, this process of exchanging worldviews is lifted into full consciousness. It called this more aware interaction Conscious Conversation.

I looked over at Wil again and said, "Conscious Conversation. Do you know what this means exactly?"

He looked at me as though I was kidding. "It's what you were engaging in when you talked with Coleman—only there was one part missing."

"What was that?" I asked.

He nodded for me to read on, and in the very next passage, the Document said the level of conversation, and the consciousness of the participants, are elevated when both people are aware of the "historical context" surrounding the interchange.

I looked back at Wil. "So it's referring to the *second* Insight of the old Celestine Prophecy?"

"That's right," he replied. "Do you remember what the Second Insight is?"

"Yeah," I said, "I think so."

I looked away, my mind drifting into an intense contemplation of the question. The Second Insight was essentially an understanding of the longer history of Western society, in particular the psychological shift that happened at the beginning of the Modern, secular age. In essence, it marked an awakening in consciousness— one we've been having trouble holding on to ever since.

The old Prophecy had predicted we would one day be able to keep this longer history fully in mind as a surrounding context for our daily activities. And when we could, this historical understanding, in itself, would completely change our individual lives. It would keep us fully awake to the spiritual side of existence.

The Modern worldview, I knew, had begun just after the fall of the dark Medieval period of history. In those times, there was no science in the West, no independent thought to speak of, and very little knowledge of natural causes. The men of the powerful Catholic Church ruled people's minds and decreed that all the events we now call natural operated solely through the hand of God—including birth, all the challenges of life and illnesses, death, and what came after, Heaven or Hell. The churchmen declared themselves the only interpreters of God's will. And they fought hard for centuries to disallow any challenge to this authority.

But then the Renaissance began, motivated by an increasing distrust of the churchmen and a growing awareness that our real knowledge of the world around us was woefully incomplete. Other influences quickly followed: the invention of the printing press, a greater awareness of the philosophies of the ancient Greeks, and the discoveries of the early astronomers such as Copernicus and Galileo, which contradicted the astronomy espoused by the churchmen.

When the Protestant Reformation occurred—a direct rejection of Papal authority—the structures of the Medieval world began to completely break down, and with them, the established reality of the people.

Precisely here, I knew, was where the Modern age began. For centuries, the churchmen had dictated a strictly theological purpose for existence and for natural events. And then that picture of life had systematically eroded, leaving humans in a state of deep existential uncertainty, especially concerning their spirituality. If the churchmen, who had always dictated the facts of spiritual reality, were wrong, then what was right?

The optimistic thinkers of that day had a solution. We would follow the model of the ancient Greeks, they said. We would commission Science to go out and investigate this suddenly new world we found ourselves in. And in the enthusiasm of the day, everything was on the table, including our deepest spiritual questions, such as Why are we here? What happens after death? And is there a plan and destiny for humankind?

With this new mandate, Science was sent to look at the world objectively and to report back. Over the centuries it wonderfully mapped the physical realities of nature, from the movement of galaxies and planets to the biology of our bodies, the dynamics of weather systems, and the secrets of food production. But it did not quickly return with an objective analysis of our spiritual situation.

At this crucial point, we made a critical psychological decision. In the absence of existential answers, we decided to turn our attention to something else in the meantime. While we were waiting, we would focus on settling into this new world of ours, devoting ourselves to the betterment of humankind. We abated our uncertainty by striving to make our secular world more abundant and secure.

And that's what we did, creating in the following centuries the greatest surge in material abundance the world had ever seen. But even as we put our energies to bettering our physical circumstances, waiting as we were for the higher questions to be answered, Science itself was pushing that higher mandate further into the distance.

In fact, as the centuries proceeded, Science began to ponder such questions less and less. In a sense, these inquiries had become a victim of Science's success in the physical realm. The more it succeeded in explaining the outer world—and created new technologies that increased the population's level of security—the less important spiritual questions became. Let the religions fight it out over the larger issues, scientists began to think. We'll stick to the physical world.

By the time the theories of Isaac Newton were filtering through Science, the dismissal was almost complete. Newton established the mathematics that defined the universe as operating strictly on its own, following basic mechanical laws, in a completely predictable manner—like a giant machine. Now, the Universe could be regarded from a completely secular perspective. God didn't move the stars in the sky. Gravity did.

The Modern, secular, materialistic worldview had been born and, pushed by Science, was exported around the planet. The idea of God, or of a deeper spiritual experience for that matter, now seemed not only unnecessary but unlikely as well. And as for the inner evidence for a spiritual reality—higher states of consciousness, Synchronicity, premonitions and intuitive guidance, Afterlife experiences—these could all be written off as pathological hallucination or religious delusion and removed from the debate completely. Even many religious institutions, suffering from diminished attendance, became ever more oriented toward secular, social activities rather than toward any discussion of real spiritual experience.

And as science and other institutions went, so did the individual. The world seemed so normal and manageable and certain that such higher questioning no longer seemed valid and it began to be pushed out of everyday consciousness as well.

Just work hard, we told ourselves, and focus on bettering your life. Enjoy all the frills and goodies of modern existence. Forget about whether knowing the purpose of life might give you higher guidance along the way, or bring more enlightened relationships with others. Just stay focused on the everyday stuff and you'll feel fine, right up to the end. If ever the prospect of death raises its ugly head, or questions squeeze into your mind about what happens after, just get busy with the secular action again until the thoughts are lost in the din.

Precisely here, I knew, we could see the real psychological truth of our longer history. We had launched Science to go out and discover the truth of our spiritual existence, and when it didn't return, we dedicated ourselves to improving our earthly conditions. And then, gradually, everyone forgot what we were waiting for. Slowly, our preoccupation with the secular world became a full-fledged, psychological obsession.

And like any obsessive behavior designed to repress something— in our case, the missing answers about the true purpose of life—it takes ever more frenzied activity to keep from remembering what haunts us.

By the time the Modern worldview peaked, sometime in the later twentieth century, such obsessive behavior had made the careers of dozens of existential psychologists, who mapped out the vast variety of ways we kept ourselves from waking up: compulsive working, shopping, decorating, arranging, eating, gambling, drugging, sexing, smoking, running, exercising, gossiping, celebrity and sports watching, and the endless search for personal recognition from others—our fifteen minutes of fame.

These obsessions could be found everywhere. And they included, especially in recent years, the most ironic compulsion of all: religious fanaticism, where people kept themselves asleep to real spiritual experience by concentrating only on the doctrines and trappings of a particular religion—even to the point of violently attempting to force these assumptions on everyone else.

Then, thankfully, as the years progressed, we slowly began to wake up. Over the past few decades, something, indeed, had popped in the collective human psyche. Why? Perhaps it was the inherent inability of repression to endure, or maybe it was the steady influence of the human potential theorists of the seventies and eighties. Another reason could have been the sheer weight of numbers of the baby boom generation, coming to peak influence in the nineties—and questioning, as they did, all aspects of human culture. Certainly, the old Prophecy found in Peru had some level of influence as well.

In any case, our preoccupation with the material life began to collapse. Like drowning men reaching the surface, we began to gasp for the air of higher meaning. Since then, in fits and starts, more people have glimpsed a new world of wonder around them. As a larger culture, we began, finally, to discover the experience of Synchronicity.

This reawakening, I knew, was the real historical context surrounding our current lives. We are waking up from our secular obsession and taking up where we left off. We want to know our true spiritual situation on this planet. And while those still obsessed with the secular might declare such a quest impossible, intuition says otherwise.

Suddenly, I realized Wil was staring at me. He had been driving along, waiting patiently for my reverie to be over. When I met his eyes, he humorously looked at his watch, making me laugh out loud.

"Sorry," I said. "It's the way my mind works."

He nodded. "So I presume you remembered the Second Insight?"

"Yeah."

"What did it say about a more truthful historical context surrounding our interaction?"

"It says we're waking up from a five-hundred-year-long preoccupation with the material and secular world, wanting to know what life is really about."

Wil beamed. "That's right. And the Document says anyone who sustains Synchronicity, and remembers the context of awakening, will be guided into a flow of Conscious Conversation. And hence will become part of a worldwide consensus-building process to discover the truth of our spiritual nature."

I looked at Wil. "Won't that take forever?"

Instead of responding, he nodded toward the rest of the Document in my hand. When I began reading, I realized I had only one page left, which was torn off at the bottom and contained only one paragraph. It said that each person who holds the truth of his Synchronistic journey, while listening for the truth in another's journey, helps to build a new, more truthful worldview. And because of this honoring of evolving truth, that person exudes a special influence on the world. All we had to do was keep our energy up.

I perked up, thinking again of the Document's reference to the last group of Integrations we would discover as a Rise to Influence.

I looked back over at Wil. "It's the centering of ourselves in truth that creates the Influence, isn't it?"

He nodded. "We'll find out once we discover the rest of this Integration."

Indeed. I had no doubt. We were only on the Second Integration, yet everything was occurring just as the Document had said it would. The First Integration showed us that expecting Synchronicity and telling the absolute truth to others kept these mysterious coincidences coming. And now the Second Integration seemed to be saying that if everyone was doing that, and thus staying awake, we would discover what we needed to know. The only things mentioned that weren't fully clarified yet were the idea of influence and the cryptic remark about "keeping our energy up."

Suddenly, Wil was pulling the Cruiser over to the side of the road.

"It's your turn to drive," he said.

*   *   *

All morning, I drove west. The big sky had stayed blue, and the sun-shine vivid, over hundreds of miles of wheat fields and pastureland. For hours I just gazed out on the flat horizon until, at one point, I felt myself get slightly bored and hungry.

Just before noon, I stopped at a roadside gas station and filled up the Cruiser with gas. Unable to resist, I bought a packaged apple pie from the counter and ate it slowly as I drove. It tasted really good, maybe too good. Within twenty minutes my head began to hurt and I felt a sudden drop in energy. The funk lasted for several hours. When Wil finally woke up, I told him what I'd done.

"Let me get this straight," he said. "You, the disciple of Blaylock, ate a mass-processed pie right off the shelf. You know better than that."

I knew he was talking about the problem with glutamates that Blaylock railed against. Glutamates, MSG-type substances resulting from the processing of various proteins and oils, are often added to processed foods, mainly because they, like MSG itself, are taste enhancers. They don't have a taste themselves, but the first bite sends immediate signals to the brain that you are eating the tastiest thing in the world, despite what are probably very bad ingredients.

The food industry says they're not harmful, but according to some experts, glutamates have been proved to inflame the brain and disrupt other organs, contributing to a myriad of modern diseases such as diabetes, Alzheimer's, and especially obesity.

"Let me guess the symptoms," Wil said. "Maybe a little nagging headache, tired eyes, low energy, absolutely no inspiration to do anything. All for a small initial hit of taste euphoria."

He shook his head. "Eating is one of the most obsessive things we do in the Modern world. If your particular feel-good distraction is food, it by definition has to taste really good, because otherwise it won't give you that pacified and satisfied feeling that comes when glutamate receptors in the brain are activated. The food makers find a way to artificially do that for you with glutamates.

"The big problem," he went on, "is not just the health impact. It's how it affects your consciousness. You can't keep your energy up and stay alert spiritually if you are drugged."

He stopped and looked at me.

"What?" I asked.

"The Document states that keeping our energy up is important to developing influence."

"Yeah, I remember."

He glanced over and caught my eye. "Food is the first level of energy we allow into our consciousness, so it's basic to integrating a higher mastery over life. And the ironic thing is that real food, the kind that's organic and pure, and freshly picked, stimulates those same receptors in the brain, and gives us just as much *natural* euphoria—without bringing us down later. Did you know that most people have never tasted a fresh-picked organic vegetable? Most of what we buy in regular stores is weeks old and stone dead."

At just this moment, Wil abruptly stopped talking and was staring at the top of an exit ramp we were passing. He shook his head.

"What's wrong?" I asked.

"There was an SUV parked at that last exit. It happened last night as well."

"You think they're still following us?"

"Not following us, just observing. They must be tracking us with a satellite or something."

"What? That would mean these people are highly connected with the government."

"That's right. But at least they don't seem to want to detain us. They could have done that anytime after daylight. They just want to know where we are going for some reason."

I looked Wil in the eyes. "You think it's the Document they're interested in?"

He nodded. "Looks that way."

For the rest of the day, we didn't talk much. I periodically felt anxious about our safety, but each time I managed to shrug it off and recover my waiting-for-Synchronicity attitude. At this point, I felt there was no alternative to pursuing this Document, at least for a while longer. The only effect I saw on Wil was that he became hypervigilant about finding clean food.

"You getting poisoned," he said to me, "was a reminder."

Every time we stopped for gas, he'd ask for the location of organic food stores and farmer's markets, and we were able to shop at several. At each mealtime, we'd exit at a truck stop and fire up the lightweight propane cooker Wil carried in his pack. In fifteen minutes we'd have enough steamed vegetables for a great, nutritious meal. After twenty-four hours of this, I felt incredibly energized and clear thinking. I could even see with greater acuity.

By nightfall we were in Albuquerque, where we eased into an enclosed garage owned by a friend of Wil's and had the vehicle and all our belongings scanned for surveillance devices. Everything was clean. Afterward, we spent the night at a small hotel nearby, which we paid for in cash, and rose early the next morning to drive to Arizona.

At midday, we began to notice the vehicles again, and by midafternoon, we took the exit to Sedona, driving right by one of the SUVs sitting in plain sight.

"They want us to see them," Wil commented.

"Who are these people?" I asked.

"I don't know. But you can bet that sooner or later they're going to tell us."

I just shook my head and tried to focus on the red rock hills we were driving through. Entering the Sedona area was always a reminder that some places are pure power spots. If you're clear enough to sense it, driving through the little town of Oak Creek, and then up into Sedona proper, is a journey into a higher world.

It feels like pure aliveness and clarity, and as you gaze out at the spectacular hills and formations surrounding the small town, you immediately feel a change in your perception. Everything around you stands out more, and the Synchronicity literally explodes in frequency, just by virtue of being in this place.

We drove slowly along the main street leading uptown, looking around at the people on the sidewalks. There seemed to be a lot of tourists and locals, and judging from their dress and demeanor, people from out of town who weren't tourists. They looked like serious trekkers who, like us, were looking for something. For a while we cruised around uptown seeing what might happen, and for a moment, I felt as though I was about to run into someone of importance. Yet nothing occurred.

Since our food had run out, I suggested we drive west toward the sinking sun and stop at the New Frontier Grocery for a salad. When we arrived, instead of parking, Wil just let me out, telling me he wanted to go look for some Hopi friends of his who lived in the area. I went in and ordered my salad and one for Wil to go, then sat down at a table in the corner to eat.

I had almost finished when someone caught my eye at the door—it was Coleman. He hadn't indicated he was coming to Sedona when we talked at the truck stop. But here he was, walking straight over to me, like a man on a mission.

"I saw you come in," he said, pulling some loose papers out of his briefcase. "Have you seen this? It's part of the Document you've been talking about."

I quickly looked it over, and indeed it was the same passages about the Second Integration I'd read earlier, but it included ten more pages I hadn't seen before.

"Where did you get this?"

He shook his head and smiled in amazement. "I hadn't been here ten minutes last night when I ran into your lady, Rachel."

"She's not my lady," I protested.

"It was just a manner of speaking. Anyway, we're staying at the same hotel. Then later, I came down to the lobby to get a cup of coffee and overheard two people talking. When I got closer, I realized they were talking about this Document.

"I walked up and introduced myself, and it turns out they are scientists. Do you believe that? And they were discussing the very question you posed earlier: how real scientists could study the topic of spirituality. And that's not all. They had the first and second parts of the Document with them and were relating it to an old Prophecy that became known years ago."

He laughed out loud. "You think my mind was blown or what? The more I talked to these guys, the more we found we had in common. We all took to one another immediately and wound up talking half the night. And guess what? Early this morning, we hiked out into the desert, and I got it! I understand that Synchronicity is real, and how to sustain it, and that we're waking up to systematically explore our spiritual nature again. They gave me a copy of the Second Integration. I wasn't surprised when I saw you again."

He was full of energy, talking ninety miles an hour about having all this Synchronicity. I chuckled. This was the typical Sedona effect that everyone talks about.

"Go ahead," he said. "Read it."

I started where I had left off with Wil's copy, finding that it continued on the same point, emphasizing the importance of Conscious Conversation for bringing in a new consensus about spiritual experience.

"Do you see what this is saying?" he interrupted. "It's not using the precise words, but my new scientist friends and I agree. It calls for applying the scientific method to our individual search for spiritual truth. Everything it says to do is what good scientists do already.

"This process has yielded all the basic laws of physical reality, from Thales to Newton to Einstein, and I see now how it can be applied to the inner experience of spirituality. For instance, consider the phenomenon of Synchronicity. Because it feels the same for everyone, we can discuss it and compare notes and reach consensus about how it works."

I was just listening, not believing I was talking to the same person. Even the basic expressions on his face were different. Instead of continuing to frown and debunk spirituality, he had experienced something he couldn't explain from his old point of view, and had snapped awake, just that quickly.

"Listen," he said. "I owe my interest in all this to you. If I hadn't said something to you at the Pub, or if you hadn't asked how Science might investigate Synchronicity and spirituality, I might never have seen the truth of it. I wasn't even intending to come to Sedona until I talked to you at the gas station."

He smiled at me, then continued. "You know, I haven't been very successful as a scientist. I couldn't keep my mouth shut. I was fired from MIT because of my opposition to commercial interests buying particular outcomes of studies. But the idea of engaging in a method of inquiry that's honest and dedicated to truth, that's what I've always been about. You've really had an influence on me."

Influence, I thought, that word again.

He nodded toward the pages I was still holding. "And this last part, it fits exactly with something I've been fascinated with for a long time, as though that part of my life was preparing me for all this."

I gave him a puzzled look.

"The Document speaks," he said, "of something Immanuel Kant advocated centuries ago with his idea of a categorical imperative."

I nodded. I knew a little bit about Kant. He was the father of a philosophy called phenomenology, which essentially called for thinkers to suspend their ordinary way of looking at a given phenomenon in nature in order to see it in a fresh way. In fact, I'd used his term *bracketing assumptions* with Coleman earlier. I'd even heard of the imperative idea—living and conducting yourself as if other people would be compelled to live and believe the exact same way as you—because, said Kant, that is the exact influence we actually have on them.

"Does the Document talk about all this?" I asked.

"No, not in Kant's terms," he replied. "But it's saying the same thing. Everyone has to not only be honest but tentative in their beliefs before making great proclamations, otherwise we can be pulling others in the wrong direction, just by this mysterious influence we have on them. The Document says that we have to come to grips with the fact that our personal reality is contagious."

He paused and looked at me. "It says each of us must first and foremost 'prove to ourselves' that our conclusions about spirituality actually work before we pass them along as truth. And because we are adding spiritual knowledge to our secular reality, we should use 'logic first' as we proceed."

He leaned closer to me and hushed his voice. "You know there are a lot of screwball ideas floating around here in Sedona."

I laughed. He was right, of course, and some of these crazy ideas were being pushed by outright charlatans, out just to make money.

But, as Coleman was learning, the effect of the place itself, the hills and streams and overall beauty, was as genuine as the light of day.

"It also says," Coleman continued, "that when we feel convinced inside that our spiritual experiences are real, then we must live them fully and openly and tell everyone about them, because if there really is an influence—and I believe there is—then it helps everyone get to a higher level of experience faster."

He was suddenly on his feet. "Keep this translation," he said. "I made copies."

"Hold on," I said. "How do you think this conscious way of consensus making is going to unfold?"

"It will come together like any other scientific consensus. First, there will be ever-larger areas of agreement, as common experiences are discussed and found to be the same for everyone. Then these will coalesce into still larger principles, as with Newton's and Einstein's theories about the secular world. Eventually, we'll arrive at certain laws governing the whole thing: the basic, natural laws of spirituality."

Without saying anything else, he scribbled his cell phone number on the top page of the Document, gave me a wink, and bounded out the door.

When Wil picked me up, I was stretched out on a bench near a grove of fragrant junipers, enjoying the first pink streaks of sunset. As I climbed into the Cruiser, the sun sank below some thin clouds near the horizon line, turning into a red blaze that now colored the clouds with streaks of orange and dark amber.

The beauty of the moment was striking. Everything around us—the sculptured peaks of the surrounding hills, the small businesses across the street, and every cloud in the sky—was cast in a pleasant golden aura. People were stopping on the sidewalks and pulling their cars to the side of the road just to watch.

Another magical Sedona sunset, I thought as I looked over at Wil in the driver's seat. He grinned back at me, and I suggested we drive over to the Airport Vortex to watch the dramatic finale there. Wil nodded in agreement and in ten minutes we were climbing a rock formation near the vortex that was shaped like a circular pyramid. At the top, it flattened out into one crowning area of rock about forty feet in diameter.

For a long time we just watched and soaked up the energy of the light. I couldn't help thinking more about the mythology of Sedona. All around the area, many believe, are special locations that have a particular uplifting effect on people. Some are large vortexes like the one here. Half a dozen or so of these have been marked and identified.

But legend has it that not only do these major vortexes dot the Sedona landscape, but other, smaller places of power are hidden about in the surrounding ravines and mesas as well, waiting for the casual hiker who chances to sit down nearby. As the mythology goes, there is a personal vortex waiting for everyone who journeys to Sedona, a spot of our own where each of us can be lifted up into consciousness and into a greater destiny. All you have to do is hike around until you find it.

I wondered, given the life clarity Coleman was suddenly displaying, if he had already stumbled upon his.

I smiled and looked out at the horizon again. Here at the Airport Vortex the feeling is about letting go of all one's concerns and soaking up what can only be described as a supportive, healing energy, a sense of being totally content and safe. I leaned back on the rocks, feeling myself letting go to it—wanting to be nowhere else besides here, in this moment, basking in the glow.

We watched the sun sink beneath the horizon and disappear, sending out a more yellowish light, and then a pale gray. I looked over at Wil. He nodded and got up, and we started down the hill. As we walked, I told Will about seeing Coleman and reading the rest of the Second Integration.

"I met with my Hopi friends," he replied. "They showed me the rest of the Second as well."

"What do you think about this idea of building a new consensus about spirituality? Coleman said it was what he was meant to do."

Wil stopped and pulled me to the edge of the trail as a group of people heading up the slope walked past us. Several of them looked us over, as if wondering whether seeing us here was a Synchronicity. We smiled back and nodded, and they walked on.

"I think that many people know," he said, "that somehow Synchronicity is calling us together to do something historical. The world is a mess, but we can fix it if we stay alert and keep our historical context in mind. We have to stay awake and help each other stay awake."

Wil was looking at me with determination, and in that moment, I felt a full elevation into the clarity of the Second Integration. How many people out there, I wondered, have noticed the same quickening? Were we already influencing one another to wake up to Conscious Conversation and to Kant's mysterious influence? And if so, where would our consciousness go next?

"What about the Third Integration?" I asked. "Had your Hopi friends heard anything about it?"

He nodded, a big smile erupting on his face. "Yes, they knew it well, although they didn't have any copies with them. It says that when people in any culture begin to wake up and hold Conscious Conversation, they quickly find the key spiritual 'principles' built into the fabric of the Universe."

"Really?" I commented. "Coleman guessed that. He said we would discover the laws of our spiritual nature. Did your friends tell you about it?"

Wil began walking down the hill again. "Yeah. The Third says these laws have already been discovered. And in order to go forward, we only have to prove them out in our own lives and then come into 'Alignment' with them. It also says in this time period, we will have extra motivation to do just that."

"What kind of motivation?"

"We have to come into Alignment," he repeated, "because it's the only way to avoid something else: a quickening Karma."

MOVING INTO ALIGNMENT

I woke up to Wil tapping on my hotel room door. We had driven to the Bell Rock Inn and checked in, and I had turned in before eleven, expecting an early departure but not this early. I glanced at the clock by the bed: one A.M.

"Wake up," Wil was whispering though the door as I opened it. Hurrying in, he handed me a large pack and some new clothes and boots.

"What's all this for?" I asked, still groggy.

Wil moved over to the window and looked down toward the parking lot where my Cruiser was parked.

"Take a look," he said, pointing.

I strained to see in the faint light. "What?"

"Our friends are back. There on the street behind your Cruiser."

It took a few seconds, but finally I spotted an SUV well hidden among some trees. Several men were gathered together beside it. One was on a radio, looking toward us.

"Yeah. I see them."

Wil shook his head. "Looks to me like they're about to do something. Put on the new stuff, and leave your other clothes and boots in the room. Someone may have placed a locator on us since we've been here."

"Wait a minute," I said. "It's the middle of the night. What are you thinking we should do?"

"We have to lose them again, which means we must leave your vehicle here. Don't worry. The Hopis will keep an eye on it. Rumor has it there's a group of people camped way up Boynton Canyon who have more of the Document. We need to get our hands on the Third and Fourth Integrations as soon as possible, and we don't want to chance being detained. We need to get deep into the wilderness."

Wil was helping me pack my new stuff and inspecting everything else I was placing in the pack. I knew the Boynton area, which was known as a sacred place and held many Native American ruins. I had tried to hike it several times but had always decided to return after only a short walk. Something about it seemed spooky.

"That's a tight canyon in places," I said. "We get up in there and we're trapped."

He gave me one of those determined looks. "There are ways out, if you know where they are."

I knew Wil well enough to know this wasn't a humorous moment. From the look on his face, he was leaving my course of action completely to me. I could come or not. And he would be perfectly fine leaving me right here.

"The Hopis consider this canyon a place of purification," he finally said. "It may be just the location to understand Alignment and Karma."

I looked at him a moment more, noting that he had mentioned Karma a second time, then said, "Okay, let's go."

We gathered the rest of our things and sneaked out the back door and across the edge of the dark parking lot into some trees. Then Wil led us through the shadows into another lot, where an old diesel Mercedes that smelled like peanut oil was waiting for us. The car was driven by a small, muscular man with long black hair. Climbing in as quietly as possible, I struggled to account for the smell. Finally, it came to me. The car was running on biofuel made from recycled commercial frying oil.

"This is Wolf," Wil said, introducing me to the driver. "He is my longtime Hopi friend."

Wolf appeared to be about fifty years of age, except for his eyes, which looked much younger and were light amber in color and very piercing, exactly like those of a real wolf. He gave me a smile and nodded.

No one talked as Wolf drove us down a few streets and then doubled back several times to check if anyone was following. We even stopped for a while, turning the car lights off, just to be sure. When everything seemed safe, we took a road that wove through a section of houses, and then entered the main road heading west out of town.

"Better get centered," Wil said, and looked away.

I knew exactly what he meant. I took a breath and reminded myself of where we were in the process. Expecting Synchronicity was now fully ingrained in me, so I focused on keeping the truth of our longer context fully in mind. Immediately, I felt more awake and alert, right on the edge of unfolding events.

After a few more miles, Wolf slowly pulled up to the Boynton Canyon trailhead. To our surprise, dozens of cars were parked all along the road. Wil and Wolf glanced at each other. As we were collecting our gear, Wil handed me a flashlight and told me to watch for rattlesnakes.

Wolf laughed and then walked closer.

"Remember," he whispered, "canyons are for purification, but mountains are for finding *Vision*."

I wanted to ask him what he meant, but Wil was motioning for me to follow him. As Wolf drove away, we headed into the canyon. After about a mile, I moved closer to Wil and asked, "Is there a larger mountain near here?"

Wil stopped in his tracks and turned to face me. "Why do you ask?"

"Something Wolf said."

"There's a large wilderness called Secret Mountain a few miles north."

He walked ahead again, then turned and added: "One aspect of Wolf you should know about—he often knows what's going to happen."

I had heard of Secret Mountain but knew only of its general location. One thing for sure, the wilderness it was part of was huge. I figured we would have to wait to know what Wolf had meant, and surprisingly, I was content to do so. I should have been apprehensive about our sudden flight into the wild, but the deeper we penetrated into the wilderness, the more energized I felt. And instead of the spooky feeling I had experienced the last time I was in Boynton, I was now feeling the opposite emotion—a sense of being at home somehow, and trusting that whatever might happen here was going to be beneficial.

We were now walking through an area of juniper and mesquite interspersed with huge red boulders and outcroppings. A sky of brilliant stars made the flashlights almost unnecessary.

"Why," I asked Wil, "do the Hopis believe this place enhances purification?"

"Because of its impact. It repels anyone who isn't ready for a breakthrough of some kind. But when you *are* ready, the power of this place helps you."

"You mean energetically helps?"

"Yes. According to legend, if you go far enough in here, say at least a couple of miles, it inevitably tests your assumptions about life and inspires a reanalysis of how you forge your way in this world. Again, it makes perfect sense that we are being led into this canyon to study the Laws of Spirituality.

"All this is up for people because of the economic downturn. During the material age, we tended to think we were creating our subsistence with our knowledge and reason, the common assumption being that if you used your head and worked hard, you could prosper in life.

"But in reality, everyone knows there are intangibles at work in determining who has success. You can be equally as logical and hardworking as the next person and not do as well. There's always been an unknown factor concerning who is fortunate and who isn't in this life, and we're about to figure it out."

He stopped suddenly and gazed out toward a flat area above the trail to the right.

"Let's go up there," he said, "and set up camp and sleep for a little while before dawn."

We made our way up to the location, and in just a few minutes we had both tents up and the food bagged and roped in a tree to protect it. Afterward, another question came to mind.

"So you think the missing factor is this Alignment thing?"

He nodded. "According to my Hopi friends, the Third Integration says that during a time of transition such as we're in, when economies are faltering and people are acting crazy, we'll all be shown a new way of getting our worldly needs met."

Wil was already climbing into his tent.

"Let's see what happens tomorrow."

The next morning, I was awakened by tree limbs breaking outside and Wil yelling. I pulled on my boots and looked through the tent flap. It was barely daylight, and Wil was running toward the tree where our food was tied. When I got there, I could see the limb was broken and the bag containing our provisions was missing.

"Did you see her?" Wil asked, pointing up the slope. "She was big."

"I couldn't see," I responded.

We looked around until we found some large tracks.

"Strange," I added. "I didn't think there were many big bears around here anymore."

Close by were several freeze-dried meals that had fallen out of the sack as the bear had dragged it away.

"We could track her," I said, picking them up, "and try to recoup some of the food."

Wil just looked at me and I knew what he was thinking. Not a good idea. We weren't armed, and that was a very large bear. Perhaps she even had a young cub.

We made our way back to the tents and Wil got out his cooker and began preparing one of the meals. A chill was in the air now, and a light rain was falling.

"The question," Wil said, "is what to do? With no food, we have a decision to make. We might have to be in this wilderness for many days. We need provisions. On the other hand, if we go back to get them, we might run into those guys following us."

"What choice do we have?" I asked.

"We could just keep going. Let this play out."

I was resisting. "We can't stay up here without food."

Wil just looked at me. "Well, it's a challenge, but isn't the same thing happening out there in the world? Think about it. Millions of people are experiencing this same situation. They go in to work one day and hear they're fired, and suddenly, no more money for food. They're in this same situation we're in now, only worse."

"But how will we eat? Are some of your Hopi friends up here somewhere?"

"No," he said. "They're already looking for the Fourth Integration farther up north. We'll have to rely on getting food from strangers."

I squinted. "That might not be easy."

"No, but again, in reality isn't that what we all have to count on? We're all in business somewhere, aren't we? Even if we work for the government, if others don't buy what we're selling, or no longer need our service, we can't survive. So to some extent we all have to be fortunate. If the Universe doesn't smile on you, if you're not lucky, then you're in big trouble. In times like these, especially, we come to realize we are solely dependent on strangers showing up to, in effect, give us food."

I'd never had it put that starkly, but I knew Wil was right. Cut to the bone, we're all always at the mercy of others.

"So it figures," Wil continued, "that there are some esoteric rules working behind the scenes determining whether people are going to show up or not—rules that we can figure out and get into alignment with. I'm telling you this because it is exactly what the Third Integration says."

"Okay," I said, "then let's see how it plays out."

Within minutes, we had consumed the stew, put the tents and water in our packs, and headed up the trail. After a while, Wil looked back at me.

"There's something else. Remember that other cultures have awakened in history in the same way we are now. These cultures have always been smaller and somewhat isolated, but they have always discovered the same basic spiritual principles that operate in this Universe."

I ran up beside him. "So you are sure the Third is going to tell us what the laws are?"

"Yes, the basic laws are known. The Hopi told me some of these principles have aspects that aren't fully complete yet, and of course, they have to absolutely be proven out in one's own life before they can be believable. But yes, we know what the basic laws are, beginning with the one we've already been using."

"What is that?"

"The Law of Truth. We used it to keep our Synchronicity going, and it governs the situation when we swap truths in Conscious Conversation. Just remember that it's easy to stay in truth when the Synchronicity is flowing to help you. It's much harder to maintain the habit when the economic stakes get high."

Suddenly, in the distance, I saw two people walking along the trail in front of us.

"There are some people up there," I said to Wil.

We sped up until we could see them clearly. Two men were walking together, dressed in hiking gear and floppy hats and bearing large, expensive packs.

I looked over at Wil. "What do you think?"

He shrugged. "They look okay to me. I don't think there's anything to worry about."

"Okay," I said, feeling for some reason I should handle the matter. "I'll go ahead and talk to them about buying some food."

Wil looked slightly surprised that I took the initiative, but smiled and nodded.

Campers, I knew, were usually extremely friendly and helpful. I was sure that, as long as I didn't appear threatening, they would share some of their food. When I reached them they both turned around. I gave them a big smile and introduced myself, and they told me their names were Paul and David from California. I knew immediately that they were tourists and probably knew nothing about the Document.

At first they seemed very friendly, but just as I gathered my thoughts to bring up the issue of food, they looked at me suspiciously and began backing away.

"Listen, something has happened," I said. "We were supposed to bring some food to friends camping up here, and our food was stolen. It's really important that we get there right away." I was pulling my wallet from my back pocket. "I was hoping you might have extra food I could buy."

"We have to get moving," Paul said, fidgeting. And his friend, David, added quickly, "There are park rangers on this trail all the time. I'm sure one will come along any minute."

Both of them were almost running up the trail now, looking back as if they thought I might give chase. They hurried ahead until they were completely out of sight.

Wil came up behind me with a perplexed look on his face.

"That didn't look like it went well," he said. "What happened?"

I was just as confused and told him every word of the conversation. He was shaking his head, smiling. When I got to the part where I had told them our food had been stolen and we needed more to take to some friends, Wil grimaced noticeably. I felt embarrassed but rationalized the fib by saying I was afraid they would think we were crazy or unstable, since we hadn't just hiked out to get more food.

Wil stared at me, remaining silent, still shaking his head in disbelief. At the same time, I realized how weak and nervous I had become. I had lost all my centered clarity.

"We were just talking about telling the truth," Wil said.

"I guess I outsmarted myself," I replied. "It really brought me down."

He looked at me sympathetically. "Once you elevate your clarity and energy in an authentic way, then it's pretty dramatic what happens when you lie about something. It's an immediate crash."

I moved over and sat down on a rock, and Wil sat beside me.

"Look," he added. "It's the canyon. It accelerates everything. It doesn't feel good, but what happened is a helpful Synchronicity just the same. You just have to see what it's showing you. During the

Modern age, we've been bending the truth for our obsessive personal gain, or to further some political end. That's why, as we wake up, we see corruption and greed everywhere.

"But as you can see, at higher levels of consciousness there's no such thing as a lie or a distortion that is okay. The Law of Truth is absolute. If we don't stay honest, to our best awareness, it hurts everyone: us individually, because it collapses our energy and clarity; and others because we fail to give them the benefit of our truth and positive influence."

He was up and heading down the trail again and I followed along.

"This brings us," he said, "to the next spiritual principle the Hopis told me about: the Law of Connection."

Just at that moment, we caught sight of a crowd of people in front of us. Walking closer, we realized everyone was looking in one direction, farther into the canyon. Then we heard the object of their attention: the sound of a helicopter in the distance.

Wil gave me a look, and we eased up slowly to where the others were. From here we could see the chopper hovering only several hundred yards ahead. It stayed there a few moments more, then slowly descended to the ground and cut its engines.

Wil leaned over and whispered, "That isn't a tourist helicopter. It's military."

Some of the people who seemed like tourists began to walk casually up the trail again. But two groups held back: us and a group of about a dozen men, all of differing cultural backgrounds. Some were clearly Europeans and Americans, but judging from their speaking patterns, most of them seemed to be from out of the country, probably the Middle East. As they moved around, I saw two women with them as well.

One of the women turned to face us, and I recognized her immediately. It was Rachel, the woman I'd seen at the Pub. She walked away then and began talking to the other woman in what sounded like Hebrew. As I watched, I suddenly felt a rush of emotion toward Rachel similar to the one I had felt before.

I quickly looked away just as Wil grabbed my shoulder. Many of the men in Rachel's group had spotted us looking at them and were staring hard in our direction.

"Let's walk on," Wil whispered.

We headed deeper into the canyon, wanting to put some distance between the men and us. Out of the corner of my eye I could see them glaring at us as we walked. Finally, when we were out of sight completely, Wil darted off the trail to the right.

"I think we should get off this trail," he said, and led us straight up the slope about a hundred yards, where we ducked behind a large rock outcropping. Once there, I felt more hidden, yet we could still see some of the main trail down below through the scrub pines and junipers. The eastern wall of the canyon towered behind us.

I told Wil I'd seen Rachel.

"Really," he said. "That was her, huh? I wonder who those people are she's with."

"They looked none too friendly," I remarked.

We waited there for a long time as more people came walking down the trail. There was no more noise from the helicopter, so I figured it must still be sitting where it landed. The question was, who was in it? And where are they now? Was it the same group that had been following us?

Finally, Wil said, "Look, I think you have to understand what the Hopis told me about the Law of Connection."

"Okay."

"You said those two guys you asked for food earlier had started to back away from you even before you began talking."

"That's right."

"Do you have any idea why?"

"Not really."

"It was because of the Connection we have with one another. It's built into our brains. The Document says that because we're all connected, we sense what others are feeling and thinking. As we progress through the Integrations, it says we will develop this sense even more. But everyone already has this basic perception."

"Are you telling me they could tell I wasn't going to give them the exact story? My intent wasn't to harm them. I wanted to give them money for their food. I just left out some of the details."

He shook his head. "It's not that they knew what you were doing exactly. They could feel what you were feeling, and as the lie you were contemplating brought you down, they felt that drain themselves, and thus became more confused and unclear—which was an unconscious signal to them that something was wrong, and that you were probably up to no good. So they backed away."

He paused a moment as if to let his words sink in.

"And this sensitivity," Wil went on, "increases as our consciousness increases. Humanity is reaching the point where you'd better not lie, even a little bit, because if you do, there will be more people every day who will be able to sense it. Lying is just not going to work much longer."

We were interrupted again as we noticed other groups walking by on the main trail below us.

"A lot of people are coming into the canyon," Wil said, suddenly concerned. "And many of them are packed for long-term camping, probably all without permits. Eventually, they're going to draw the attention of the park rangers. We'd better find out what we can before they show up. Time to move."

He gave me a serious look. "Keep your eyes open. Watch everything that happens."

We carefully walked down to the trail again. There was no sign of Rachel or the group she was with. As we walked slowly forward into the heart of the canyon, we began to notice people sitting around talking everywhere. We found a spot out of the way and stopped.

"Listen," Wil said. "I feel I should walk up ahead alone and see if anyone knows what that helicopter is about. If you'll watch the packs, I'll go do that, and be right back."

I nodded and sat down. Staying here was fine with me since I wanted to think more about the Law of Connection. If this was a true principle of our spirituality, it meant that it was the same for all of us. How far could we develop this Connection with each other, I wondered. Would we eventually become telepathic? For a long time, I pondered what that would be like.

Suddenly, I heard someone walking up behind me and turned around to see an upbeat man of about thirty smiling and offering me his hand.

"I'm Jeff," he said. "How's it going?"

I shook hands with him and introduced myself. At first, I felt a slight downturn in my energy, but the more he talked enthusiastically about how beautiful everything was in the canyon, the more I began to think he was okay.

At one point, I even asked him if he knew anything about the Document, but he said he wasn't aware of it. After we talked a bit more about Sedona, he said, "I see you have a knife. I wonder if I could borrow it for a few minutes." He was pointing toward my belt at my prized eight-inch hunting knife that I always carried in the woods.

"We're setting up camp over there," he continued, "and I just need it for a few minutes to cut some rope."

I looked through some mesquite and saw two men and a woman in that direction putting up a tent. Figuring he would be close where I could observe him, I took off the knife and gave it to him in the scabbard—then watched as he walked back and began working with the two people.

A fresh breeze was blowing up, and I took a breath. The morning rain had cleared and the sun was beaming down. Slowly, I felt myself recovering my lost energy and noticed how beautiful this particular area was. Small pine trees and junipers dotted the entire canyon floor.

Just then Wil came back and sat down beside me.

"No one seems to know what the chopper is doing," he said. "I kept my distance from it, but I could see it was empty. And it's definitely military."

He was sitting on his pack. "Let's just wait here for a while."

I smiled. "You could tell me about the next spiritual law."

As Wil formulated a sentence, I again looked over toward the campsite where the man had been working, only to find that he was nowhere to be seen. I jumped up and ran to the campsite and asked the couple where he was. They told me they didn't know, that he wasn't really part of their party.

"He just came up to talk," the woman said. "He offered to go borrow a knife for us, to help us cut some rope. He seemed to be a little down on his luck."

I was about to go look for him when Wil came up, and I quickly filled him in.

"He stole your knife?" Wil remarked, a look of wonder and amazement on his face, as if something important had happened. I brushed it off and proceeded to look all around the area. There was no sign of him anywhere. After about twenty minutes, I returned to where the packs were, finding Wil sitting patiently, waiting for me.

"I've had that knife a long time," I said, sitting down next to him.

"Well," Wil offered, trying not to grin, "you wanted to see how all this would play out."

I was in no mood for analysis. I just wanted my knife back, but Wil was persistent. "Right before you saw the guy was gone, didn't you ask me what the next law was?"

I remained silent, still sulking.

"Well," he continued, "it's the Law of Karma."

It was past noon, and Wil had left again, telling me he was going to look for food. For a long time I just sat around, wondering what kind of purification was going on here in this canyon. Then, about the time I was ready to go look for him, I saw Wil coming back. He sat down and looked over at me.

"Find some food?" I asked.

"Yeah, a little bit. I had lunch with some people I met. I wanted to bring you some but there wasn't enough."

I just looked at him.

"Why shouldn't I find food?" he responded. "I have *good* Karma!" He was using an overly dramatic tone to his voice, then burst into laughter, barely able to control himself.

As usual with Wil, his humor was so contagious I couldn't help but laugh, too.

"Okay," I said. "What did the Hopi tell you about Karma?"

Instantly, he was serious. "The Document says that it's real, and in our time, it responds to our actions more quickly than ever before."

"So I'm the poster child for it."

"Well, take a look at what has happened. You tried to steal food from someone, and that created a karmic response from the Universe that resulted in some guy stealing your knife."

I began resisting again. "What about him? Maybe he's just a serial thief."

"Maybe, or maybe he's a nice guy and he decided to move up the trail somewhere or go back to town, and he just forgot to give back your knife. Either way, you have to ask why this happened to you right now, just when we're talking about all this and right after *you* tried to steal from someone."

"Wait a minute. Stop saying that. I wasn't trying to steal from anyone."

"No? Didn't you tell a lie in order to try to manipulate someone out of his food? Trying to do it and doing it is the same thing karmically."

"The Document says that?"

He nodded and then stared at me for a long time.

"Look," he finally added. "These laws seem hard to believe because we've all been trained to think the Universe only has physical laws. And the reason people are slow to put this together is that we all shade the truth at times, especially in business, or to save face, and we all have things happen to us that are bad. So there seems to be no relationship between the two. We think it doesn't matter if we lie a little bit, because bad things happen to everyone anyway."

He looked at me hard. "But according to the Document, that isn't true, and anyone can prove it to himself by just being observant. Because Karma is speeding up, the consequences from an untruthful manipulation come back very quickly."

"But why is it speeding up?"

He stopped. "I don't know. I asked the Hopis the same question, but they said the Document didn't say. They only hinted it may be part of the energy that the Calendar is pointing to."

"You mean the Mayan Calendar? What do the Hopi know of that?"

"The classical Maya were Native Americans, too, you know."

"Anyway," Wil continued, "prove it to yourself. The Document says that when enough of us realize this is the way Karma works, it's going to lead to a new era of Integrity to replace the corruption we have now.

"And there's more. It's important to see that the Law of Karma is designed not for punishment, but to affect a positive correction. It apparently works this way: the Universe is set up spiritually to support and encourage our spiritual growth. If you center yourself in truth, then your Synchronicity will soar. If you participate in untruth, then you draw into your life a person who does the same thing to you, again not as punishment but to show you how it feels, so you can move back toward truth.

"What happens," I asked, "if we don't get the message?"

"The Document says the response of Karma gets more extreme in an effort to get our attention, something, again, that we can also prove to ourselves at this moment in history. All we have to do is pay attention to what happens in relation to our own behavior."

"Okay, what if one is randomly selected and murdered by a serial killer? Is that payback for something we did earlier?"

"No. Remember, Karma has nothing to do with payback. It reflects back to you what you're doing. If you are an armed robber, for instance, you are standing for the untruth that says that behavior is okay. It's the same as a lie or deception to get the money, only worse. And you will have money taken from you to show you how it feels, so you can change. The problem is that some people just use the Karma as an excuse to keep the same behavior going, thinking everyone is doing it to me, why shouldn't I do it to them as well? They're missing the fact that they are being shown something so they can change.

"When someone becomes the victim of a serial killer, unless the person is a serial killer himself, it's a matter of being in the wrong place at the wrong time. It's the result of chance, not Karma, and happens because of the current state of the world's imperfection. We know psychologically and genetically what's going on with serial killers, from studies of childhood trauma and genetics. In the ideal, someone would have noticed these factors and intervened with the person early, so he wouldn't have been able to hurt anyone. Unfortunately, we just aren't enlightened enough to institute those kinds of interventions yet. Hopefully, one day we will be."

"I guess, until then, we have to hope we're lucky."

"Yeah, at least until we can move through the Integrations enough to realize we can be 'protected.' "

"What do you mean, *protected*?"

Wil leaned toward me. "My Hopi friends told me that these kinds of random accidents and mishaps aren't supposed to happen. The Document says that, as spiritual consciousness rises, we will learn how to detect the hunches and premonitions that allow us to avoid impending accidents and attacks. They said we'll get to that level at the Fourth and Fifth Integrations."

Abruptly, we heard the raspy engines of several ATVs coming up the trail behind us. In the time it took to grab our packs and duck into the thicker brush, they were driving up.

"Those are Park Service four-wheelers," Wil shouted, leading us farther up the slope away from the noise. As we hurried away, we could see people scurrying for cover everywhere. Once near the canyon wall, we saw two men up ahead attempting to climb the steep face of a wall of rock.

"They're sport climbers," Wil said, urging me along. "They probably have permits."

Suddenly, as we watched, one of their rope anchors ripped out of the rock, flipping one of the climbers upside down and threatening to drop him fifty feet to the jagged rocks below. Then another anchor broke free and dropped him another ten feet. He screamed in terror.

Without thinking, I dashed toward the cliff. The second climber was pointing frantically toward something on the ground near their tent. I immediately saw a full length of extra rope. I picked it up, then quickly made my way up the rock and out on a ledge to within ten feet of the helpless climber.

I threw his buddy the end of the rope and he knew exactly what to do. He put the end through a solidly hammered anchor near him, pulled it through, and lowered the end to his friend—who, despite his panic, was able to tie it around himself. After that, all I had to do was hold my end of the rope tightly to secure him from falling any farther. After a minute, he was able to cut himself loose from the other ropes. With the help of Wil, I lowered the man safely to the ground.

As we gathered up our stuff, the traumatized climber was so upset he was unable even to talk. His friend gave him some water and spoke with him privately for a minute, then pulled us to the side. We could hear the four-wheelers all over the canyon floor below us, but the climber seemed not to notice.

"If you hadn't come by," he said, "I don't know what might have happened. I've got to get him back to Sedona. I wish there was some way to repay you."

Wil and I glanced at each other.

Then I told them the truth of our situation, that we needed food.

"Well," the climber said, "we can sure help with that. We were going to stay here for four days, but my friend is too shaken. He wants to leave tomorrow. We have lots of food you can *have*."

After packing the food, we left hurriedly toward the northeast and found another place where we could hide in the rocks. From there we had an even better view of the canyon floor, where people were being detained or turned around by the rangers. I looked hard for the group Rachel was with but couldn't see any of them.

"We should stay here for a while," Wil said, "until all this dies down." He was still giving me that look of astonishment over what had occurred.

"I know. I know. All this means something," I replied.

"Means something? It's the most pointed run of Synchronicity I've ever seen. Remember when we were driving away from the Pub and I made all those moves to lose the car behind me, and you thought the speed of the Synchronicity was amazing? Well, you're now operating at just that level of speed.

"Think about it. You were shown the Law of Truth when you tried to manipulate for food. You were rejected by the tourists in a perfect illustration of the Law of Connection. Then, right after, you had something stolen from you, through similar false pretenses, illustrating the Law of Karma. And now you've just secured our food, which is what you were trying to do all along."

I looked at him, not quite getting the last one.

"Don't you see?" he pressed. "You aided those people by intuiting immediately how you could best help. It came to you how to help, and you did it, fast."

I knew he was right. I didn't really even think much about the actions. Somehow, I just knew.

"It's called the Law of Service. And again, it's built into the way the Universe operates and how our minds are designed. We somehow know what others around us need, and when we act in response, we fall into alignment with this law. All you have to do is think, 'How can I be of service?' And something will always come to you. All the resources you need will be provided in order to help, and you'll feel like you're always in the right place at the right time to make a difference."

He paused for a moment and then asked, "Do you see now what

the Third Integration is, in total? It's all about getting into Alignment. And again, you proved it to yourself. You played it out right here in this canyon. And anyone else who observes sincerely can see it just as clearly in his or her own life.

"It's the next step in our awakening. Like I said, during this material age, we have grown to think a little lying, a little shading of the truth, is okay, even expected. It's a dog-eat-dog world, right? Salespeople are trained to practice shading the truth. Politicians get elected doing it. Contracts with fine print are a way of life.

"Yet think about the world right now. Corruptions are immediately found out. Scandals erupt daily. The swindlers get swindled. This is what happens when most of the culture is bombarded with a Karma that is coming faster and faster. It's there to show us the imperfection so we can do something about it.

"But once you begin living the best truth you know and see that being of service to others and setting a good example are the best things you can do for yourself, well, everything changes. You move into Alignment with the way the Universe is designed to operate. You stop manipulating, and so you no longer draw manipulators into your life.

"In fact, the opposite occurs. When you seek Alignment and think how to be of service, you begin to draw people into your life who are there to help *you*. And then your Synchronicity and your dreams really take off.

"When everyone gets this, the human world will immediately change. Businesses will change how they operate. Doing business in Alignment means always telling the truth about your products and always being service-minded. And if you do, others who need what you offer will show up mysteriously."

I had never seen Wil this excited before. I thought about the idea of tithing and asked him about it.

"That's just part of being of service," he said. "Money is only a form of stored energy, and it follows the currents of Karma in one's life. If you manipulate for money, you get manipulated out of money—or suddenly have a wave of breakdowns and unexpected expenses. Tithing is a way to right the ship quickly. Instead of spending every dime, deny yourself a little and save ten percent of your income one month.

"Then just wait for an intuition of whom to give it to. You'll get one. Someone who needs an angel will cross your path, and you'll get the thrill of having the means to be of service. And again, it will just accelerate the flow of help coming back to you. You'll get more opportunities to be successful."

He stopped and looked at me. "I've never known anyone who tithed in this spirit who didn't prove to themselves that it works."

For a long moment, Wil and I just looked at each other. I knew he was feeling the same sensation I was: another rise in consciousness and energy. We had fully integrated the Third step, and added one more piece to the puzzle of spiritual reality—Alignment.

"Did the Hopis," I asked finally, "say anything about the next Integration, the Fourth?"

Wil nodded, his face turning serious. "They said the Fourth Integration is perhaps the most important part of 'the foundation,' because it will show us what is fully at stake. Once we're able to stay in Alignment, in truth, we will see how pervasive some systems of untruth are in the world.

"We can't go forward until we understand these growing ideologies and see how dangerously they are polarizing. Only then will we know how to separate ourselves from this untruth...and break through to a place where we can stand up to it."

RECOGNIZING IDEOLOGY

We stayed in the rocks, watching everything that was happening down at the trail. Our plan was to hide there until dark and then figure out where to go next. From Wil's description, it sounded as though the Fourth Integration might be challenging and more dangerous. Maybe it was the effect of the canyon, but the prospect of danger didn't disturb me as before. I was fully into the journey now. I put out the expectation for more Synchronicity and held the context that we were discovering the reality of human spirituality, vowing to stay in Alignment.

Suddenly, Wil sat up, straining to look up the slope toward the canyon wall. A group of people were walking about a hundred yards away, heading farther northeast. As they moved through a grove of small pines, we saw it was the group that included Rachel. She was next to last in line.

As I watched her, she immediately stopped and looked down the hill in our direction. Although unable to see us, she seemed to be sensing we were observing her. A tall man with a beard, walking behind her, said something and pushed her forward pointedly.

I looked over at Wil. "Did you see that? She's being held against her will."

"Looks that way," Wil responded.

I could tell he knew there was some link between Rachel and myself.

"Listen," he said, "I think I should go up there alone and see if I can get close enough to hear their conversations. They'll see us if we both go."

I knew Wil had been trained in surveillance, so I nodded in agreement.

Wil was lightening his pack, handing me some of the food.

"If I don't come back by nightfall," he said, "I'll find you later. Okay?"

He slipped over the rocks and headed up the slope. For a long while I just gazed in that direction, catching sight of him a few times as he crept between the outcroppings and trees. Then he was gone.

After a few minutes, someone talking down by the trail attracted my attention. Four rangers were walking in my direction. I grabbed my pack and slipped around the rocks in the opposite direction, hoping to make my way back toward the cliff face where the climbers had been.

Suddenly, someone grabbed my arm and jerked me to a standstill, sending my pack flying ahead of me and causing me to lose my footing. A large man with sunglasses and trekking pants stared down at me. Another man walked up from behind him and leaned forward, then politely lifted me to my feet.

"Remember me?" the man said in a British accent. "Where's your friend, Wilson James?"

I immediately remembered him as the blond man who had been observing me at the Pub.

"Wil left," I replied.

The rangers came up, and the man gave them a look. They nodded and headed back down the hill again.

"No matter," the man continued. "You two are pretty slippery, but I want you to know we wish you no harm. We're trying to help you."

He pulled me over about five feet to where the others couldn't hear. "We don't have much time. But I'm going to tell you something. You must listen very carefully. We know about the release of this Document, and we know you're looking for the rest of it. We're very interested in what it has to say, and we want you to keep searching and tell us everything that you find out."

He gave me a look that was only slightly menacing.

"Who are you?" I asked. "Who are you working for?"

He smiled. "Let's just say I'm speaking for a group that exists at the highest levels of every Western government."

I was struggling to hold on to my clarity. "What could you possibly want with an esoteric document like this? It's about spirituality."

He looked at me a long moment, perhaps aware that he could not win me over without giving me more information.

"I want to trust you," he said. "This release about spirituality is occurring at a time when the war between religions is our most dangerous problem. And don't be fooled. That's what it is, a war between those having primarily one religious view in the West, and those countries, primarily in the East, that have another view. This war may seem quieter on some fronts, but underneath, the tensions are accelerating. We have the best minds working for us, and they're all convinced we are on a downhill slide toward total destruction.

"The problem is simple. It's the old issue of the Cycle of Revenge. Every time we kill one of theirs, ten more join the fight. And every time they kill one of ours, there's a call in high places to do something more drastic to protect ourselves. There is no middle ground here. And the worst is yet to come. The whole conflict is about to go nuclear."

He stepped toward me. "Do you know the religious affiliation of the President of Iran? He's a member of a sect called Twelvers. They believe that Armageddon, the war that is prophesied to destroy the world in the last days, is a good thing—because they think when it approaches, their version of a Messiah, who they call their Twelfth Imam, will come out from the clouds, vanquish all their enemies, and then create an ideal world based on their beliefs.

"Just to show you how crazy it is out there, we find similar views among Judeo-Christian fanatics in the West. They also think that Armageddon is desirable, since they believe it will bring forth their Messiah figures to likewise defeat their enemies. Some people in both camps seem to think it is their duty to actually bring about this great war.

"This kind of fanaticism seems to reflect a growing tendency to give up on this world. People everywhere are hanging on to their religious doctrines at all cost, thinking the rest of the world is going insane. And they're hoping God will intervene to end the misery."

He looked genuinely worried.

"Don't you think," he continued, "that it's strange how the Iranians are talking, even after everything the Israelis have tried? Iran is much further along in its nuclear capability than anyone thinks. And many of its bases are far underground. That's why even bombing attacks don't deter them. Some analysts think they already have nukes now, and they're just working on the delivery systems."

He reached over and handed me my pack. "I don't claim to know what's in this Document you're studying. It seems like a bunch of talk to me so far. But we know the reputation of Wilson James. If this Document has a real solution, we want to know about it."

He gave me a serious look and added, "Otherwise measures are going to be taken by our group that no one is going to like."

In spite of the threat, I began to think he was being sincere with me.

"Don't worry about getting in touch with us," he replied. "We'll find you. We have people in every department of your government, so we have everything we need to keep up with you."

He paused and looked at me for a long moment.

"There's one more thing. This giving up on the world is not just happening in religious circles. It's happening in the political realm as well. Both Left and Right are quickly polarizing into more dangerous groups, who also think the world is collapsing, and thus they are justified in their extreme action. It is another reason we might have to act. So you want to make sure you align with us in this matter."

With that, he shook my hand forcefully and told me his name was Colonel Peterson, then reached into a satchel on the ground and pulled out some papers.

"Here's part of the translated Document we found," he said, walking away. "The Third and Fourth Integrations. Some of the people we interviewed told us more of it was rumored to be north of here, near a larger mountain."

For a long time, I just huddled there among the rocks, my head buzzing from all this. The sun was now blocked by another thick layer of clouds, and an ominous cool wind began to blow from the north. I opened my pack and pulled out a windbreaker. Now, at least, we knew who was following us. And if he was correct about the geopolitical situation and people giving up on this world, maybe this was why the Document had been released at this time.

I wondered suddenly, in the interest of truth, whether I should have told Peterson about the men who seemed to be holding Rachel against her will. Probably not, I figured, since I didn't know for sure if that assumption was true. I thought for a moment about reading some of the two Integrations Peterson had given me, but I found I couldn't concentrate. I was getting antsy—I had to do something.

Finally, I decided to move ahead in the direction Wil had traveled.

"Expect Synchronicity," I reminded myself out loud. "And stay centered in the truth of what you're doing, and in Alignment."

I proceeded carefully up the canyon until I noticed another trail that bore to the right through a rocky gap toward the northeast. The trail looked to be rarely used overall, but it contained dozens of fresh human tracks. Following them, I proceeded to another large mound of red rock where I could survey the flats farther to the north.

About a quarter mile ahead, I could see a small clearing where many people seemed to be camped. It was just across the line into the area Wil, and now Peterson, had talked about: the Secret Mountain Wilderness. The multiridged mountain towered in the distance. Camping, I knew, was expressly forbidden in this wilderness. Whoever all those people were in the clearing, their party wasn't going to last very long.

As a gray dusk descended, I hiked down the slope and into the flats. Here the terrain was less rocky and much more green, dotted with large areas of junipers, and large oaks. Several rabbits flushed from the rocks as I walked.

When I reached the clearing, I couldn't quite believe how many people were there. From where I stood, I could see at least two acres filled with campers. Dozens of people were walking around. It was as though someone had organized a music festival of sixty people two miles out in the desert, in a spot where everyone had to hike to. In reality, it seemed to be a totally spontaneous gathering, born of rumor and a desire to find out about the Document.

The larger reality of what might be occurring struck me. Ostensibly, the pieces of these writings had been dispersed all over the world. Was something like this gathering happening in many other places, all at the same time?

Suddenly, I could hear the low whine of a four-wheeler far back in the distance toward the canyon, and I knew the rangers were about to move this way. Hurrying ahead, I picked out a spot near the east side of the clearing, figuring I could make a quick getaway into the junipers when the rangers came. Around me was the glow of eight or ten campfires.

I cooked up some soup on the stove and ate it, waiting for complete darkness, and then I ventured out to see if Wil was here, or Rachel. For half an hour or so I walked around, glancing at the people and listening to their conversations about the Document. Different groups were trading copies and talking about their experiences with Conscious Conversation.

For the most part, I was ahead in the Integrations compared to those I was listening to, and I didn't feel the urge to engage anyone. I wanted to cruise around first and see who was here. After a long time, I had completely checked out most of the sites, except for several larger groups near the southern edge of the camping area. The first one included at least twenty people, all camped together.

In the center of the group, a small gas camping lantern hung from a tree, flooding the area with an odd yellow light, like the bug lights you see on porches out in the country. Moths and dragonflies eerily circled the lantern.

As I walked closer, I almost ran into another man who was entering the camp at the same time. We actually had to stop to avoid crashing into each other. I paused, wondering if this meeting was a Synchronicity.

"Excuse me," he said, in a friendly manner.

"That's okay," I replied.

He gave me a second look. "Hey, I saw you back at Boynton. You must be looking for the translations."

"Yeah, that's right."

"Where did you come in from?"

I could tell he was sizing me up for some reason.

"Georgia," I said. He introduced himself as Robert, from Idaho.

"From Georgia, huh?" he commented. "Some people in our

group are from there. We have all of the translations through the Third Integration."

At that moment, another man walked up and handed him a cup of coffee, and Robert asked me if I wanted one.

"Sure," I replied, certain now that I was being shown something important here.

We walked over to the fire and sat down, and I was handed a cup of coffee that was very hot and smelled wonderful.

"It's terrific that this Document is coming out now," Robert said. "The country is in great danger. Maybe this will get people motivated. I'm pretty sure the government will be declaring martial law pretty soon, and people need to be prepared. The first thing they'll do is take up all the guns and many books."

It was becoming clear that I was talking to someone on the extreme Right politically.

"Wait a minute," I said casually. "None of that can happen. There are constitutional safeguards."

"Are you kidding?" he reacted. "One or two more Leftist judges, and that won't be the case anymore. Things are out of control. The country we grew up in is being changed. We have to do something now. We think the Document is going to call for a real rebellion against the Leftists."

"What?" I said forcefully. "I can't see anyone getting the idea of a rebellion from this Document—maybe a more enlightened Centrism. Have you read it?"

"Much of it," he said loudly. "Our people are studying it more closely now. They'll let us know about the details. You may not believe it, but things are about to degenerate quickly. You had better decide who you want to side with when it happens."

Several other people in the group heard him and began to walk toward us.

"Everyone has to wake up," he went on. "The Leftists are slowly undermining the Constitution by overregulating. They're taking advantage of this financial crisis to consolidate power."

He stopped and looked hard at me.

"I think you're overstating reality here," I said. "There was a swing to the Left that occurred during the crisis, when more of a safety net and consumer protection were demanded. But if anything, there's been a turn in the other direction since then."

He suddenly stepped back and began to look at me with more suspicion.

"Well, boys," he said to the others, "I think we have a Lefty right here."

Before I could respond, several other people jumped in with their own thoughts on the subject, basically echoing the first man's point of view and arrogantly emphasizing my naïveté. As they continued, I began to feel slightly confused and off center and no longer wanted to argue with them.

So much for this being a Synchronicity, I thought. Best to leave now.

"Look," I said, walking away. "Everything you are saying can be debated, but you're not open to that. There is another side to all these issues." I set the coffee cup down on a rock.

Robert was laughing now, but some of the others were giving me intimidating looks.

"You better wake up," one of them yelled. "You people on the Left are ruining this country, and we're not going to stand for it much longer. We'd rather have the corporations take over than you idiots."

Walking back to the tent, I could feel my clarity of mind finally coming back to me. I had no idea that the extreme Right would have an interest in this Document, if indeed it was a genuine interest. More likely they were just trying to use it for their own purposes. Most upsetting of all was the fact that my energy had collapsed. I felt I had held on to a more rational view with them, which I considered most truthful, but I had definitely been affected by the verbal onslaught.

Then it dawned on me. These people were controllers, in the same sense that the Old Prophecy had described them in the Fourth Insight. We had come to the Fourth Integration—so of course I would be running into controllers!

As the Prophecy had shown, controllers were not interested in truth, and only marginally motivated by outcomes. What they wanted above all was the feeling of power that comes from dominating others. In order to do this, they make up any facts necessary to throw the other person off balance and undermine his self-confidence. And if the controlling was successful, the victims would eventually lose their centered clarity altogether and begin to defer to the controllers' opinions—which, of course, would give the controllers a hit of energy and power from the others' attention. Controlling is obsessive behavior, used to push away *insecurity*.

This type of controlling is the chief characteristic of those both Left and Right, who have a primarily ideological approach to politics. They don't want to debate the issues. They want only to shout down the opposition and win. The old Prophecy predicted that this selfish insecurity could be resolved only when one found true security: a spiritual connection inside, where seeking the truth and being of service were more important than winning.

Shaking off the experience, I continued to look around for any sign of Rachel and Wil but saw no one I recognized. I was about to head back to the tent when I heard someone talking in a loud voice in a campsite to my right. I looked around and tried to see through the dim, flickering light. The night was now draped in a slight fog-like haze from the smoke of the campfires.

Finally, I spotted four or five people standing in a group, illuminated by a large campfire. Two men were opposing each other in a heated interchange. One of them was shouting, and the other man was...Coleman!

I was so glad to see him that I rushed over and stood just to the right of him for support.

"You're one of those Right-wingers," the loud man said, waving a finger at Coleman. "If you weren't, you wouldn't be talking like this."

Coleman shook his head. "I'm only saying that it takes a balance. Some people want big government totally regulating everything and others want big corporate influence and very little regulation. I think the best position is right in the middle, with just enough regulation to provide adequate consumer protection."

His opponent wasn't listening, going off on a tirade about how those were just code words for Right-wing intentions to undermine programs for people. He called Coleman a fascist extremist out to control the economies of the world and oppress anyone who wasn't rich.

At that moment, a lightbulb went off in my head. We were now seeing the reverse of what I'd experienced earlier. When I tried to discuss politics with the Right-wing guy from a more moderate position, he called me a Leftist. And now I was witnessing a man on the extreme Left—because Coleman was also coming from a moderate position—accusing Coleman of being from the extreme Right.

Both extremists were using the same tactic. If someone disagreed with them even slightly, they were simply pushed into the opposite extreme category—so they could be dismissed and dehumanized and not taken seriously. That way, each side—far Left and Right—could justify their own extreme behavior. Each thought of themselves as the good guys having to fight to save civilization from a soulless enemy.

As the other man continued to shout, Coleman gave me an exasperated look and nodded that we should leave.

"Where are you going, Right-winger?" one of the other men shouted. "You aren't going to win. If we have to install a dictator, we'll do it. You aren't going to win!"

Once we were out of sight, Coleman stopped and pulled a copy of the Fourth Integration from his pack.

"We need to talk," he said.

As we walked back to where I had set up camp, I gushed out everything that had happened, including experiencing the Third Integration, seeing Rachel and the strange group she was with, and listening to the far Right guy acting just as irrational as the guy Coleman was arguing with on the Left.

Coleman listened and busied himself with picking up some dead mesquite limbs. Several times he paused to tell me he had had similar experiences with the Third Integration, not from losing his food but from being alone and losing his way and seeking help from others. We were both at the same place: in Alignment and beginning to seek the Fourth.

When we arrived, I used some starter wood Wil had placed in my pack to build a small fire, listening at the same time for any sounds that might indicate rangers were approaching.

Coleman was watching me, growing more excited. "Have you seen what the Document says about the Fourth yet?"

"Not yet."

"We're seeing all this for a reason! The Document says that during the transition from a material worldview to a more spiritual one, civility is the first thing that goes out the window. Those holding on to the old worldview often begin to cling to their obsessions with ever greater ferocity, until their beliefs become an ideology, a system of ideas that aren't based on truth any longer. It is based on the perceived idea that there is an enemy out there threatening the world. And in such a dire situation, they feel it is okay to give up on truthful democratic debate and legal procedures.

"The political Left and Right are both moving to the extreme because each thinks the threat is so great from the other side that extreme measures need to be taken. And of course, it's all self-reinforcing. When people exaggerate the facts, they abandon truth, and then the Law of Karma kicks in, and each side draws in their opposites who are lying as well, and they just fan each other's flames.

"What's worse," he went on, "is that those in the middle—as we just saw—are constantly accused of being extreme by both sides, so gradually everyone tends to be pushed toward the extreme opposite poles."

He poked the fire with a stick. "The Document says the danger lies in this increasing polarization of political thought, with more people moving to the extremes every day. This is a very dangerous situation. Either side can become violent or despotic. The Document says those in Alignment must find a way to stand up to those in extreme ideologies by creating a new, enlightened center, devoted to the truth. It says this is especially true when confronting religious ideology."

I just looked at him.

"I was very interested," he said, "when you were telling me about the group Rachel was with."

"Why is that?"

"Because the Document says religious ideology will also be increasing in our time. In this period where many people want an open discussion about spirituality so we can build a consensus about our spiritual nature, many in established religions will begin to feel threatened. And in an effort to defend their doctrine, they will move to extremes as well, even to the point of giving up and wishing for the end of the world."

I remembered what Colonel Peterson had told me.

"You're talking about the end-times people," I said. "Those wishing for Armageddon."

"Yes."

Just at this moment, the low whine of four-wheelers interrupted our conversation. They were still far away but were bearing down on us at a fast pace. People everywhere were hurrying to break down their tents and gather their belongings.

"We'd better get out of here!" I said, jumping up and loading my pack.

"I'll get my tent and be right back," he said, rushing into the darkness.

Just then, I was jolted by a woman's scream about fifty feet away. Several men with big flashlights had grabbed her and were looking all through her belongings. Several more men were heading my way.

With no other choice, I stuffed everything into my pack and ran into the darkness. All over the area now, I could see men with flashlights searching through people's campsites, obviously looking for something. I crouched low as one group of men rushed into a camp less than thirty feet from where I was hiding. Beams from their lights swept over me.

"Let us have your translations," one of the men said in an Arabic accent. Another shouted to an associate in what was clearly continental Indian. I recognized one of the men as belonging to the group holding Rachel. He was the tall man with a beard.

Now the four-wheelers were on us, and the men quickly scattered, the flashlights suddenly going dark. I moved away from the rangers, looking around as best I could for any sign of Coleman. Finally, I hid among some rocks about a hundred yards away. Dozens of rangers were herding people into groups and moving them out of the clearing. I headed farther north.

After about an hour, I froze. Someone seemed to be creeping toward me from the left. The sound stopped, and I backed away in the other direction and right into the grasp of a lone figure who pushed a handgun into my ribs. I was wrestled to the ground by another man, and one of the big flashlights popped on in my face.

They pulled me along for about a half mile farther toward the north into an area of thick pines, where more than twenty people met us. A small campfire flickered light over the scene. This was the rest of the group that had Rachel.

A man who seemed to be the leader came over and gazed at me for a long moment. He was thickly built, had dark hair that was graying, and was dressed in military fatigues. He shook his head and turned away. I took a deep breath, trying to keep my wits about me and stay out of panic. After all, I told myself, Rachel had been with these people for a while, and she hadn't looked too upset earlier.

On the other hand, they had just come into the clearing and had terrified everyone, apparently looking for parts of the Document. I could see folders and loose papers stacked near a lone cactus. One man walked over and began searching through my pack, easily finding my copies.

Suddenly, two other people emerged from the darkness. One was Rachel and the other was an Arab male of about thirty-five who was attired in more formal Arab dress. Rachel moved closer and saw me, our eyes meeting for just an instant before our view was blocked.

The leader then walked over and casually sat down in front of me.

"Where are the rest of your Documents?" he asked. It was the same man I'd heard speaking with a continental Indian accent.

I was determined to stay centered and to be truthful or say nothing. "That's all I have," I said.

He gave me what I could only describe as a serene smile. "Okay, my friend, then where might we find the rest of this artifact?"

"I don't know. One has to be guided to it."

"And you, are you guided by Colonel Peterson?"

I was stunned, which made the leader's eyes light up. He was obviously pleased with himself that he knew of the colonel's existence.

"Oh, yes," he added, "I know all about his group. And I want you to tell me all you know about him."

"That's easy," I said. "I only met him for the first time earlier today, and I don't know anything about him, except that he's interested in what this Document has to say, just as you apparently are."

"Yes, we're studying it right now," the leader said. His eyes tellingly glanced at Rachel, who was sitting beside the stack of papers.

"So what about you?" I asked. "What do you think about this Document?" He seemed to be amused that I would dare to ask a question in this circumstance.

"It has nothing to tell us," he asserted. "We already have the truth."

He turned and began talking to the well-dressed man who was with Rachel. He called him Adjar.

At that moment, Rachel looked directly into my eyes, which was so overwhelming I had to shift my gaze. The connection wasn't romantic—at least I thought it wasn't. But it was definitely unusual, and I felt it at depths I had no idea how to explain. As I looked at her with my peripheral vision, I realized she was trying to communicate something.

Cooperate, she seemed to be saying with her eyes. Don't make waves. Which threw me into a quandary. To stay clear, I had to remain centered and aware, and to do that I had to tell the truth as I knew it. I would have to phrase my truthful comments in a way that would keep me out of trouble with this guy.

The leader was walking back toward me.

"This idea of ideology," he said. "It refers to people who are living lies and know it, yes? Like those who lie and steal for money, like you people in the West."

He looked closely to see if I was going to defend Modern life, but the thought came to me to go in another direction.

"I think the Document is pointing," I said, "to those people who have set ideas about reality and aren't open to any discussion about it. They stop growing and just repeat the past. They aren't conscious in their conversation."

"Like Peterson?"

"Well, I don't know."

"You know!"

For the first time he looked fully menacing, and I knew I was on tricky ground here.

"Okay," I said. "I think he is trying to find a way to stop the war over religion before it's too late."

He looked as though he was trying to control an inner outrage.

"He only wants power for himself," he said. "Besides, the war cannot be stopped. It is destined. I think you are trying to deceive me."

With that he turned away again. Rachel was staring at me, cautioning me to be careful.

The leader looked at Adjar. "Set a guard over them all night."

Adjar nodded to two other men who lifted me up and had me sit by Rachel, then he said something to the other woman in Hebrew. She moved over to a rock about ten feet away to watch us, an Uzi machine pistol in her lap. He called her Hira.

I leaned over toward Rachel and noticed her rose perfume again, which in this setting made her seem otherworldly, or angel-like.

"Who are these people?" I whispered.

"I've been with them a while," she said quietly, "and I still don't know much about them. They mostly belong to Arabic sects, but they have Westerners with them, too, Jews and Christians from all over. The only connection I can see is that they are all into end-times Prophecy. The leader's name is Anish. He's the one who holds them all together."

I quickly told her what Peterson had said about religious extremists desiring Armageddon.

She thought for a moment. "I know Anish is planning something. I just don't know what it is. They call themselves Apocalyptics."

"And they won't let you leave?"

"I haven't pressed the issue. They made me agree to help them understand the Document, although only a few of them are comprehending it." She glanced over at Adjar who quickly looked away.

I took a breath and then told Rachel about the men terrifying the campers at the clearing.

"I was thinking they might be forcing people to give up their copies," she said.

She looked at me, trying to find my eyes again. "How far have you gotten with the Integrations?"

"I'm through the Third and some of the Fourth."

"So you get the problem with polarizing ideologies, and the disregard of moderate views?"

"Yes."

She seemed to light up. "Well, the conclusion of the Fourth is revealing. It says there is only one solution to the problem of people who are lost in ideologies. The Document says those of us in Alignment, holding a central position of truth, have to *reach them*."

"What does that mean?"

"It explains that enough of us have to move through the Integrations until we have enough influence to persuade them, before it's too late, that Alignment is the only way. People can change in the blink of an eye."

"A race against time," I said.

She gave me a puzzled look.

"Just something a friend told me when I first heard about the Document."

At this moment, the leader, Anish, walked up and said something to Adjar. Then he gave me a long look. He seemed to grow irritated that I was returning his stare. He stormed over.

"Who are you to look into my eyes?" he yelled. "Show deference! You are here, alive, both of you, because I allow it. When you no longer serve our cause, I can dispense with you in an instant." He snapped his fingers to illustrate the point.

Then, strangely, his demeanor became calm again, and he smiled. "Tomorrow, you will tell me everything you know."

He glared one more time at both of us and walked off.

The threat was convincing, and I felt my energy plummet. Rachel looked at me hard. She glanced at our guard, Hira, who returned her look with concern. Hira jumped down from the rock with amazing athletic ease, ready for whatever was going to happen. Rachel nodded at her.

I realized then that Rachel must have developed a friendship with this woman with the Uzi. In fact, Rachel seemed to have a Connection with both Hira and Adjar. After she was sure he wasn't coming back, Rachel leaned over again, still searching for my eyes.

"There's one last thing in the Fourth," she said. "All of us must admit that we can't marshal enough influence on our own to stand up to such people. It says we have to break through to a larger part of ourselves...and find our 'protection.'"

THE GOD CONNECTION

I sat alone, staring at the dying fire. The well-dressed Arab man, Adjar, had returned and talked for a long time with Rachel as they gathered up the copies of the Document.

Afterward, he supervised as I erected my tent, then escorted Rachel to her own tent, leaving me alone except for Hira, our guard, and three extremists who were sitting together on the far side of the camp. Occasionally, the men would burst into muted laughter as they smoked cigarettes and took turns drinking from a bottle of wine.

My mind was spinning over the situation. My energy had crashed, and I had no idea what to do. I thought momentarily of the Document's idea of finding Protection but found no help. Whatever was intended by that word would remain a mystery until something happened in my experience to give it meaning. Until then it was just one more abstract term.

Looking again at Hira, I figured I could make a run for it and perhaps get away, but that move would leave Rachel here alone, and I wasn't going to abandon her. Hira looked around suddenly and stared hard at me, and when our eyes met, her look shifted into something akin to curiosity or inquisitiveness, but only for an instant.

Something in her look made me feel better, and I thought about trying to speak with her but decided against it. The day had been long, and in spite of the fear, an irresistible fatigue was descending on me. For a few minutes I looked out into the night and tried to conjure up an expectation of Synchronicity. Then I crawled into my tent, literally unable to stay conscious. Where was Wil? I wondered. And Coleman?

I was awakened by the muffled sound of conversation outside my tent. At first, I thought I was dreaming, but then I heard Rachel's voice distinctly. I glanced at my watch. It was an hour before dawn.

"Don't you see?" she said in a loud whisper. "We have to figure out how to bridge our differences."

I peaked through the tent flap and could see Rachel outside by the fire. Adjar was sitting across from her. The rest of the camp was dark and silent. Hira was no longer on the rock.

Rachael was pressing. "Spirituality cannot be forced. People must discover it for themselves."

He was shaking his head. "What we believe is that culture must be shaped and kept spiritual. The spiritual rules must be maintained by those in charge. Otherwise, our people would be spoiled and lazy. Look at the indecency and degradation of your movies and music. And you hold up your corrupt politics as something to be proud of?"

"Look," she argued, "I don't like parts of our culture, either. But freedom is important, for men *and* women. What if the Document is correct? You understand what it says. You've experienced the Alignment. What if people everywhere could learn to practice a spirituality that establishes the discipline you speak of, but is voluntary and engaged in because of the thrill of the experience?"

Suddenly, Hira returned with an alarmed look and began speaking to Rachel in Hebrew. Adjar looked as though he wanted to strike her, but he turned and walked a few paces away in disgust.

I pushed through the tent flap then and startled them all. Rachel shot me a look of grave concern and walked over to Adjar.

"Some of the others have opened up to Hira," Rachel whispered to Adjar. "Anish is saying he's not going to let us go! You have to help us get away!"

Adjar said nothing.

"You know what the Document is saying," Rachel pressed. "It says we can experience a Breakthrough of some kind. We have to figure out what that is. It could lead to a resolution between both sides. What if Armageddon doesn't have to happen?"

Adjar turned away again, as though under terrible stress.

Finally, he said, "Okay. Get your belongings."

Hira ran up to Rachel, her gun hanging from her shoulder, pointed to herself, and said something, which seemed to mean she was going with us.

Rachel turned and looked at me, smiling as though thoroughly astounded that her plea had been granted. I whirled around and began dismantling my tent as quietly as possible. Within minutes, the three of us were carefully walking to the north. Behind us, Adjar was standing motionless watching us go, the firelight glistening on his tall forehead.

"What about Adjar?" I whispered to Rachel. We were climbing up the steep, wooded incline in the direction of Secret Mountain.

She stopped and looked back at him.

"I don't know," she said.

Rachel found a break in a steep outcropping where we could make our way to the right along a small ridge. Suddenly, we heard a loud sequence of yells and arguing behind us at the Apocalyptics' camp, apparently at the discovery of our absence. I could see the large flashlights come on again and a group of men begin heading our way.

We hurried our pace toward the north, ever deeper into the Secret Mountain Wilderness. This area, I knew, was at least forty square miles of rough terrain. We walked until well after sunrise, and at each rise in the terrain we stopped to rest and to check if the extremists were following us. Each time we would see them still back there but not catching up.

As the sun rose higher in the sky, we quickened our pace until we couldn't see them anymore and then pushed forward into the early afternoon, when we virtually collapsed from exhaustion. We set up camp on a rise of rock surrounded by thick bushes except on one side, which allowed us a view down the ridge.

For the rest of the day, we ate camp stew and took turns keeping watch and sleeping. Finally, we all gathered on the edge of the rocks to watch the sunset. Rachel sat down beside me, and Hira sat a few paces away, watching for movement and still appearing very nervous. As the sunset unfolded, swirling cirrus clouds picked up the last of the light and began to look like little pink Angels.

"I guess they were protecting us back there," Rachel said.

I nodded.

"You're still going to need them!" Hira suddenly shouted.

A hundred yards away, a group of seven extremists were jogging up the hill toward us. Some of them had assault weapons on their shoulders.

"Come on," I said. "We have to get out of here."

In minutes we had grabbed everything and were running up the slope toward the top of the mountain, scaling rocky outcroppings and making our way through thick clumps of trees. Hira had moved in front of us and was directing the route.

"Let her lead," Rachel said to me. "She used to be in the Israeli military."

We were making our way around one of the tight ledges when my foot suddenly slipped and I felt myself toppling off the edge toward another spire of rock twenty feet below. At the last second I leaped to a boulder about ten feet down and slid to a prone position, scraping my arm on the jagged rocks.

"Are you all right?" Rachel was whispering from above.

I could see there was no way back up to her.

"Yeah," I said, "but I'll have to find another way up. I'll meet you ahead somewhere."

She nodded, and I took off. Glancing behind me in the descending darkness, I could see the flashlights of the Apocalyptics flickering on again and bobbing up and down as they closed in on us. Suddenly, a single shot rang out, reverberating against the mountain in a series of echoes that chilled my soul.

Despite everything I could do, my energy began to fade even more. I sought to bolster my consciousness by telling myself how important it was to make it through this, to find the remaining Integrations. I even tried to expect Synchronicity again and to somehow seek Protection, but I knew full well that there was no one out here in this wilderness to come to our aid.

I was running through the darkness now, jumping from boulder to boulder. At one point, to my horror, I found I had no way forward without moving back down the slope in a direction closer to the bobbing lights. Worst of all, up ahead, the slope ended in a sheer rock face. I would have to climb virtually straight up the rocks to get away.

Another gunshot rang out, which threw me completely into panic. It all seemed meaningless now. Now there was only fear, and the desperate desire to get away.

When I reached the rock face, I chose the best way I could see and climbed for my life. At each ledge of rock reached, the lights flickered erratically over me, telling me the men were climbing as well. Were they already sighting in on me with their weapons? The thought sent me into ever larger waves of panic until the level was simply unbearable. At that moment, I began to feel the resignation of imminent death descending on me like a wet blanket, sapping my remaining energy. My legs began to feel like lead.

Then suddenly, I was buoyed by a memory. This exact circumstance had happened to me before, years ago, during the search for the Prophecy in Peru. I was in the exact same situation, giving in to death as a respite from terror. Back then, I had opened up to a consciousness I hadn't experienced before or since.

With that thought in mind, I regained some of my balance and climbed to the top of the rock face. Then I squeezed through a narrow opening between two large outcroppings, attempting to find a way up to my right. To my shock, I found myself totally blocked off and stymied by a sheer drop-off ahead of me. Again, just as in Peru.

Rocks sliding down the slope behind me told me the extremists were close. My rubbery legs began to fail again, and I slumped to the rocks. Again the blanket of surrender began to cover me—only this time I didn't fully let go. A part of me, the part that remembered the experience in Peru, didn't give in. I moved into a zone where I was the pure observer, the detached witness, there only to watch the unfolding drama that would determine my fate.

Taking a breath, I looked out at my surroundings, waiting, and then, just as in Peru, something began to change. Without investment, I watched as my consciousness suddenly enlarged and reached out to everything around me, giving me an odd feeling of familiarity, as though I was recapturing a natural part of myself that had been lost.

Instantly, my perception was filled with everything I hadn't noticed before: Small moths and flying insects circled around my head. Crickets, or perhaps grasshoppers, sang their song from the trees and rocks. I became aware of a large bird, perhaps a hawk or owl, awakened by my rude intrusion, which cried out and flew away. I could hear each thump of the wings, as if it was flying off in slow motion.

Above me, the sliver of moon that had guided my way was now hanging lower in the sky. As I looked at it, I felt another expansion of my being, one I also remembered from before. No longer was it merely an artifact in the sky, two-dimensional in its appearance, like something seen on television.

This sliver was now perceived by the observing part of myself in a larger way, so that I knew in my perception that the phases of the moon are really a change in the way the sun's light reflects off the moon's round, three-dimensional shape, hanging there in space.

The perception stretched my awareness even more to include not just the moon but the sun as well, hanging, as it was, underneath Earth's western horizon and shining upon the moon. The effect was to extend my sense of space past the local area around the ledge I was sitting on, out to the larger cosmos in all directions—and not just over my head and to each side. I felt it under my feet on the other side of Earth as well.

With that, everything was suddenly thrown into greater relief, a kind of super three-dimensionality that enhanced the presence and realness of everything in my perceptual field, from the small insects close to my face all the way to the galaxy of stars behind the moon. I was looking at everything from the larger perspective of the entire Universe.

Everything around me came alive with an overwhelming beauty and majesty. The rocks and trees virtually glowed with color as every reflection of light outlined their contours and crevices with multicolored reflections. The large pine tree that bordered the ledge to my right seemed to explode with a thousand variations of red and blue highlights.

As if pulled on by my growing sense of beauty, I then felt myself expand at the emotional level into a profound feeling of love and Connection with everything around me. Something in the area of my heart burst outward, and I knew without a doubt that I was now home and cared for, and absolutely—I couldn't believe it— Protected.

For a while I merely soaked up the emotion, but then my image of myself as a person began to shift. Somehow, in this moment of euphoria, the witness part of myself could now see all the events of my life as one long movie. I could see all the Synchronicities, all the thoughts and ideas that had come to me at just the right moment in my past to guide my life forward—revealing now a hidden purpose behind it all. I could see that all I had done came from a truth I had come into the world to tell. But I could also see that my truth was part of a larger, hidden truth, a Plan for all of creation.

This recognition lifted me into still another, even larger emotional opening. The love, the euphoric sense of being at home, of being involved in a Universe of higher purpose, were all still there. But along with it was rising a profound sense of appreciation for this Connection and support. It was like suddenly realizing that some Divine force had been behind me all along, without my fully knowing it—and now was suddenly jumping from behind the curtain, yelling "Surprise!"

Only it was more deeply heartfelt than that. To understand, at this level of illumination, that I was part of something larger and older and longer was almost overwhelming in its impact.

And here, in this moment of appreciation, something else also seemed to be occurring. I was sensing some personal point of Connection from which this love and belonging emanated. What was this? When I tried to analyze it, it simply disappeared altogether. Yet when I concentrated on feeling the love and well-being and appreciation, there it was again. It was as if appreciation completed a circuit of Connection somehow and brought the point of contact closer.

For a very long time, I just sat there, somehow feeling everything at once, the heightened perception, the love and well-being, the sense that there's a Plan toward which we are all being guided, and finally, this elusive point of Connection I couldn't understand. I didn't want to move.

The night sky had vanished in the first light of dawn, and everything around me was standing out even more in vivid color and distinctiveness. Suddenly, I felt my attention being pulled down the slope. Gradually, I realized I was hearing human voices. I leaped to my feet so effortlessly it amazed me. My body was moving differently, not just with more energy, though that was true, but also with more coordination and precision. Squeezing through the boulders again, I quietly moved back down through the rocks, realizing the voices were coming from a point a hundred feet or so to my right, behind some trees. When I came close I could hear the accents and knew it was the Apocalyptics.

Without fear, I moved slowly to my right so that I could look down on them. Anish and the tall bearded man were talking loudly. Behind them were Rachel and Hira, and a larger man sitting on the other side. When he turned, I realized it was Coleman, and he looked terrified. Anish and the bearded man were arguing over what should be done with the three prisoners.

"They know what we're going to do," the bearded man said. "To release them would threaten our project."

"What do they know?" Anish said, glancing at Rachel. "Nothing that can hurt us. The end is approaching and no one can stop it."

The bearded man looked angered. "We can't keep taking chances like this. What are we doing here on this mountain, anyway? This idiot Document means nothing. Why are we looking for more of it? We have to get to Egypt."

Anish turned his back.

"I have to insist," the bearded man said forcefully, "or we must go our own way." Several armed men stepped forward from behind him.

"No, no," Anish said. "Our coalition is too important for that." He looked over at Rachel with a hint of pity.

"You don't want to do this," Rachel said. "The Document will explain the end times, what all the Prophecies really mean. I know it. We can all find the truth together. It could bring peace."

At this moment, I understood in a flash that all of us—Rachel, Adjar, Hira, Coleman, myself, and Wil, wherever he was—were here for a reason. We were part of the Plan. We were in the right place to intercede with these extremists somehow. We could learn to reach them, as the Fourth Integration said. But how?

The idea suddenly came to me to move farther to the right and try to create a rock slide that wouldn't hit anyone but might create enough of a disturbance to allow our group to escape. I was about to do just that when I caught sight of someone else in the exact area I had in mind. Suddenly, a huge rock cascaded down toward the pines, jarring other rocks loose, including one the size of a bathtub. As the roar started, the Apocalyptics began running in the opposite direction.

I knew I somehow had to get Rachel and the others to run toward me, and I felt myself spontaneously go into a state of intention, akin to prayer, only it wasn't just me. I could somehow feel a Connection to many others who were helping. Who were they?

Almost on cue, Rachel grabbed Hira and ran through some rocks in my direction. As our eyes met, Rachel slowed for a moment and seemed to stagger. Hira saw me, too, and grabbed Rachel's arm to keep from stumbling. Last to see me was Coleman, who held on to to a rock for balance. I could tell they were being lifted into the same consciousness I was in.

Rushing through the blinding dust and confusion, I grabbed Rachel and Hira and led them back the way I'd come. Coleman was right behind us. Rocks were continuing to crash down the slope, and as we ran I looked up toward the source of the landslide and noticed movement again. I pulled all of them behind another outcropping near a large tree, where we couldn't be seen. They were smiling up at me, feeling no concern about the dangers.

Abruptly, someone peeked around the tree and looked at us— Wil. The sight of him lifted my awareness even higher, and when he looked at me, I knew he was also in the same consciousness as the rest of us.

"Follow me," I said spontaneously. "I know where we can go."

I quickly led them back up to the outcropping where I was earlier and through the narrow passageway onto the ledge. Rachel, Hira, and Coleman still seemed to be consumed by their state of consciousness and found separate places to sit down.

Wil and I walked back outside to keep watch.

"You started that rock slide, didn't you?" I asked.

Wil nodded.

I laughed. "I thought about causing a rock slide myself, but you thought of it first."

He looked at me and said, "Who knows? Maybe you thought of it first, and I heard you. Or perhaps we thought of it at the same time. That's my guess."

I knew he was referring to the Connection we now all seemed to have with one another.

I took a step toward him. "Do you think these extremists will...?"

Wil completed the rest of my thought before I could get it out: "Follow us? I wouldn't be surprised."

He made the comment without alarm, as though he hadn't a care in the world. Which seemed odd given our circumstances, until I realized I felt exactly the same way. We were thinking and acting in hyperspeed, doing what we had to do. But part of what we were feeling—the love, being home, guided by some mysterious intuition—was definitely the constant sense of being invulnerable, as though nothing could happen that we wouldn't be able to handle or be guided through.

I looked at him. "You feel the Protection, too, don't you?"

At this moment, I suddenly thought to look down the hill. Wil was already moving past me to do the same thing, climbing higher on the outcropping to get a good view. I was right behind him. When we got in place, we could see movement. A small group of men were heading up toward us, weapons in hand.

"I knew it," he said, rushing back to the ledge.

So did I, I thought, trying to keep up with him.

As we moved through the opening, something else came to mind. When I was out on the ledge the night before, it was dark. Maybe there was a way off the ledge and down the hill in that direction after all. When we arrived, Rachel was already looking over the ledge with Coleman, searching for that exact thing: an escape route. All of our minds seemed to be working together in some kind of super Connection.

Coleman was now totally in sync.

"What is happening to us?" he asked, smiling. "I knew the Fifth was about having a Breakthrough, but I never expected—"

"Just concentrate on the sense of Protection," I said instinctively.

His face told me he understood.

"There's the way," Hira said abruptly. She was looking over the right side of the ledge. "We can drop down to the next rock and move along the slope to the right."

I moved over and looked. "That's a fifteen-foot drop!"

"You can do it," she said.

Turning around, I could see everyone getting their gear ready. Wil gave me a "let's go" look.

Hira was first, dropping her pack and then jumping beside it like it was nothing. Coleman dropped his belongings to Hira and then crept out to the end of the ledge and hung momentarily by his arms before dropping. Wil did the same thing. Then Rachel walked over to me and I took her by the arms and held her over the ledge. As I did so, our eyes locked into the deepest Connection I'd ever experienced, as though our souls touched.

I held her there for a long moment and then dropped her easily to the others, before jumping down as well. As I dropped, I thought of something I'd long forgotten. All my life, since I was very small, I'd fallen periodically, sometimes from great heights. Once, when only three, I thought I could fly and, with an apron tied around my neck like a Superman cape, had swan dived off an eight-foot retaining wall, landing unhurt.

Later, as a youth, I had climbed a twenty-five-foot extension ladder over a concrete floor to help put up a light. The foot of the ladder suddenly kicked out and I fell the entire distance to the floor, landing on the ladder precisely, with my hip and shoulder each hitting a rung in the ladder so as to break my fall—the only way possible to have kept from being seriously injured. I walked away unharmed.

And finally, I'd fallen in college. While working as an electrician, I fell from the attic of a shopping center through the ceiling of a jewelry shop below, landing squarely on top of an eight-foot glass display case and shattering my way through four glass shelves until I bounced to the floor. When I landed, I carefully removed dozens of swordlike glass shards lying all across my body and got up—again, without a scratch.

During every one of these falls, time had slowed down and a sense of certainty had swept over me that everything would be all right, the same feeling I was having now as my feet landed on the rock below. I wondered if I had tuned in back then, somehow unconsciously, to this same sense of Protection.

Hira led the way and we found a route that took us around a large ravine and back down the eastern side of Secret Mountain. As Hira kept up a good pace ahead of us, I noticed she was rock hard and muscular, like a gymnast, and now bursting with enthusiasm.

"Don't fall behind," she said at one point, but even before she spoke, every one of us had instinctively begun to pick up the pace.

After about a half mile, we had come down to the flats northeast of Boynton Canyon. There I began to get tired, and the euphoria and clarity seemed to be wearing off. Hira stopped for a minute, allowing us to catch our breath. As she looked at me, her face was different, as if she was suddenly worried again. I looked at the others and was met by newfound expressions of concern. Clearly, everyone was coming back to normal again. I looked back up toward the mountain.

Without warning, another gunshot echoed across the desert, throwing all of us into panic again. We were in the last of a group of small outcroppings before the terrain opened into a large, flat area of mostly desert. We huddled low in the rocks, facing a dilemma.

Behind us somewhere were the Apocalyptics, and ahead of us were two hundred yards of open ground before we reached a stand of junipers that would provide some cover. We could either run straight across or go to the right, where thicker pines and rocks offered more cover.

Wil was up ahead, crawling back to me.

"Are you holding your centeredness?" he asked.

I looked at him and shook my head. "Just barely."

"Remember," he said, "that what just occurred was a Breakthrough, a glimpse of a consciousness that we now know is possible. But we'll have to work our way back to it."

Just then, several more shots rang out, striking the rocks fifty feet away. The Apocalyptics didn't know exactly where we were, but they were still behind us. Everyone was crawling over to Wil and me.

"They're shooting from the ledge where we were," Hira said, her voice shaking slightly now.

"What are we waiting for?" Rachel said. "We should just run straight across to the next hill."

"Are you crazy?" Coleman said. He was looking up at the ledge. "I can see two or three of them. All with weapons. There's more cover to the right. Use your logic."

As he talked, an image of us running to the right crossed my mind, and then my level of energy seemed to crash even more. I looked at the route straight ahead and it seemed better for some reason. I was certain that going in that direction was the right option.

"What do you all think?" Wil asked.

"I think we should go forward," I said.

"What?" Coleman said. "Not me. They'll cut us down."

Everyone looked at Rachel.

"I think forward," she said.

Coleman shook his head, then took off to the right, running through the junipers and darting from one spot of cover to another. Seconds later, the rest of us began running straight across the open space, spreading out the best we could as we zigzagged.

Suddenly, a hail of bullets rang out in the direction of Coleman. Looking back, I could see that some of the Apocalyptics had taken a position on the hill directly above him and were pouring fire straight down in his direction. Everyone was slowing down, looking back in his direction.

"Go! Go!" Wil shouted, just as the gunmen on the cliff opened up on us. Bullets began to kick up soil to our left and work their way toward us. At that moment, I caught Wil's eye, and for the first time ever saw a look of resignation on his face that we might not make it. And then I felt again that same feeling while falling as a youth, that everything would be okay.

Suddenly, we could hear the roar of a helicopter flying toward us. When it was almost directly overhead, it tilted in our direction, and I could see several men in the back compartment. One of them was Peterson. He recognized me and did a double take, just as several more shots cut up the ground closer to us. Realizing what was happening, Peterson began motioning to the pilot, and the helicopter sped ahead and buzzed the Apocalyptics on the overhang. The firing stopped.

"Let's go!" Wil yelled, and we all ran until we came to the first red rocks of the next hill. Once there, we looked as the helicopter circled the extremists a few more times and then left.

"How did the chopper know we needed help?" Hira asked.

"They didn't know," I said. "They just happened to be flying by."

She gave me a puzzled look.

"It was a Synchronicity," I clarified. "We were protected."

THE GREAT COMMISSIONING

After three hours of tough hiking, we made it to the first paved road. Earlier, we had waited a long time for Coleman, thinking he might try to get across to where we were. We even thought about going back to look for him in case he was hurt, but we found our way blocked by a host of police cars and Forest Service jeeps racing in a cloud of dust toward the mountain. We were all tired and shaken except for Wil, who was buoyant about what had happened.

"You know," he said, at one point, "all that happened was showing us exactly what we needed to see. I haven't seen a group of people spontaneously open up to an experience like that ever. The Document says we can't handle violent ideologies alone, that we need to have a Breakthrough and find our Protection, and that's exactly what happened."

I nodded, too fatigued to comment.

"There will be plenty of time to rest in Jerome," he added. "And I have a feeling Coleman is okay. We'll find him."

Jerome, I knew, was an old mining town west of Sedona, now favored by artists.

"Why there?" I asked.

He gave me a smile. "That's where the Hopis are waiting for us."

Without talking any more, we caught a ride with a rancher to the nearest pay phone where Wil called Wolf, and within about twenty minutes, he arrived in the same Mercedes. As we all piled in, he caught my eye and grinned at my dirty clothes.

"Have any visions?" he asked, snickering.

I nodded, then collapsed into the backseat. Wolf took us up to the hilly mining town and then past it about a mile to a small homestead. The house was adobe, covered by a new tin roof with solar panels built in. Across from it was a pole barn and corral, holding three well-groomed horses. A flock of chickens scattered as we drove up.

We were greeted by two other Native Americans, an older woman of about eighty and a teenage boy who looked fifteen. They quickly served us a huge meal of corn fritters, chicken, and guacamole with onions. In an hour we had showered, eaten, and sleepily erected our tents, barely saying anything. By sunset we had all turned in.

I slept without dreaming and didn't awaken until a ray of sunlight shone through the flap of the tent and hit my face. A chorus of birds sang in the small cottonwoods over my head. As I pulled on my boots and crawled out, I saw a fire and sat down beside it. For the first time, I noticed that the landscape sloped away from the house to an acre-size pond bordered by another very large cottonwood. Several crows cawed from a rocky area beyond.

Looking out at the landscape, I felt as though the past several days had been a dream, and I was back to my old self. I deeply needed the cup of coffee the young boy handed to me.

"What's your name?" I asked him.

"Tommy," he said in perfect English.

I nodded toward the older woman who was standing nearby. "Is she your grandmother?"

"Yes."

"What's her name?"

"Grandmother."

"That's her only name?"

He nodded.

Just then she called to him and he ran over to her and hung on to her neck, beaming back at me proudly.

I sweetened my coffee with some honey from a jar sitting in a basket near the fire and then sipped it slowly, not wanting to think about our experiences. I knew there would be plenty of time for that later. Right now, I wanted only to sit and appreciate the simple beauty of the place and feel the normalcy for a while. A crow suddenly flew over the corral and landed on a post nearby to stare at me. I shook my head and looked away.

"Up already?" Rachel abruptly asked from behind me. The timbre of her voice was slightly different from when we were on the mountain.

"Yeah," I responded, standing up. When our eyes met, I blushed for some reason and avoided her eyes again, as if we had just had a one-night stand or something.

She sat down on a burlap cushion near the fire and the boy served her coffee as well. Reaching into her sweater pocket, Rachel pulled out a dollar bill, which he at first refused to take, glancing at his grandmother. Rachel insisted and he smiled widely and stuffed it into his jeans.

As I watched Rachel, some of our experiences on the mountain forced their way back into my consciousness, at least intellectually. I knew I'd experienced what could only be called a Divine Connection, and real Protection, along with a deep interaction with Rachel and the others. But I knew, as well, that much more had occurred that I couldn't recall.

I remembered Wil saying it was a glimpse into what could be, one that we would have to work to regain. I still didn't know what that meant. After a moment, I let go of all the thoughts, suddenly feeling vulnerable, and began to consider leaving. My logic told me enough was enough. A group of extremists had just tried to kill us, and even though we had escaped, why tempt fate any longer?

Suddenly, Rachel slid her cushion closer to me and said, "All that occurred back there was important."

"Really," I replied, not sure I wanted to hear it.

She gave me an upbeat look. "The Document says that the opening to the God Connection happens much more frequently than most people think. It's also structured into the nature of the Universe and into how our minds work."

Her smile was beguiling, so I flowed with her train of thought and considered the work of Jung again, wishing Coleman were here. The Swiss psychiatrist, I knew, had discovered more than the phenomenon of Synchronicity. He was also famous for his notion that our brains and minds were structured by archetypes.

He thought humans, for instance, were able to learn to walk without thinking about every individual muscle involved because the pattern of muscle coordination necessary for this activity was already built into the structure of our brains—contained in what he called preestablished archetypal pathways that were genetically passed down.

To walk, we had only to see others walking and try it ourselves, which fired up the pattern of neural pathways that help us learn the activity quickly. Because these pathways are basically the same in everyone's brain, learning to walk feels exactly the same to all human beings.

Jung argued that spiritual development was structured in the same manner, in a latent pathway that was waiting for us to fire it up. And again, this experience feels identical for all of us.

"So much happened yesterday," I said finally. "It's hard to get a handle on it. And I can't seem to get back that feeling we had on the mountain."

She looked at me with excitement. "Yes, but the Fifth Integration says we don't have to remember it. We just have to keep on integrating the remaining steps and we'll rise back into it—you know, the Rise to Influence the Document talks about. The only part of the experience that we can keep now, as part of the Fifth Integration, is the sense of love and protection."

"That's what Wil said," I remarked, nodding for her to tell me more.

"The Fifth Integration is completing what the Fourth set up," she continued. "If we intend to hold the truth and stay in alignment in the face of the most dangerous ideological untruth, something opens in our brains to honor that. We know we can't face this kind of danger by ourselves merely with our own strength of ego. No one can. Yet that recognition fires up a pathway that's already there, and we experience a Breakthrough—one that gives us a Divine Connection, and the premonitions and Synchronicity necessary to be protected."

I nodded. The feeling of Protection was coming back to me. Until now, horrible things happened to people at random because we didn't have the consciousness necessary to hear the warnings that could steer us clear of such danger.

If the Document was correct, Protection seemed to be a natural part of our innate spiritual ability, growing, I supposed, out of the Law of Connection. With this thought, an image came to me of the future. Would humanity someday be so aware of our premonitions that we would all know, for instance, to leave a city for higher ground just before a tsunami or earthquake arrived, just as the animals do?

Rachel was staring at me.

"Next for us," she said, "is to begin to systematically recapture the experience we found on the mountain so that we can begin to live it every day. We're at the Sixth Integration. Remember the Prophecy found in Peru? We're going to discover a mission."

She turned a little, trying to look into my eyes again. I lingered just a bit longer in her gaze before turning away.

Suddenly, Wolf was pulling up to the house in his car, and we jumped to our feet to meet him. Surprisingly, he had Coleman with him, and another man in the backseat I couldn't see. We hurried to the car and finally caught sight of the man's face. It was Adjar.

Wil came out of the house, and Wolf told us he had found Coleman with the other scientists in Sedona. He, too, had escaped when the helicopter had distracted the extremists. As for Adjar, some of the other Hopis in town had spotted him at a medical clinic. Wolf said Adjar had been able to escape after being interrogated by the extremists.

"Unfortunately," Wolf added, "even though the police were well aware of the extremists' presence, none of them were caught."

"Did you hear that?" Hira responded. "That means they could be coming up here right now. We have to do something."

"What is the matter with you?" Adjar burst out. "Can't you just be at peace for a moment?"

"That, coming from you!" Hira screamed. "You people are the great destroyers of peace!"

Rachel immediately restrained Hira, and Grandmother led Adjar toward the house. For the first time, I saw that Adjar had a large cut on his forehead and was holding his arm.

Wil was looking hard at Wolf.

"Where is that place you told me about?" he asked.

"Down there by the pond," he said, nodding, "near the large tree. We call it the place of harmony."

"Good," Wil replied. "We're going to need a lot of that."

For most of the day we rested and ate our meals alone. Adjar never came out of the house, and Hira was mostly silent and reserved. After telling me briefly about his experience of being captured by the extremists, Coleman slept virtually the whole day. He seemed distracted, as though he was working on something and had to go through his process before telling me about it.

As for me, I was totally obsessed with the idea that our Breakthrough experience was built into each human brain. If this notion was true, then it might mean that all the Integrations were built into the structure of our brain as well, and hence were in some sense destined for all humanity. I busied myself reviewing the Fourth and Fifth parts of the Document, which corresponded exactly with what I had been told.

About dusk, I turned around and saw Adjar and Hira talking with Wil. At the beginning of the discussions both were raising their voices and turning their backs on each other. Toward the end, however, the two spoke together for a few minutes with no rancor. Eventually, all three walked down to the big cottonwood and joined Wolf, who was throwing wood on a large bonfire built in the center of a circle of logs. I knew Wil and Wolf were planning something. You could feel it. There was a palpable sense of expectation in the air.

I headed that way myself, and on the way I walked by Rachel's tent. She came out carrying a little journal and smiling at me, as though we'd set a specific time to get together.

"I wanted to make a few notes," she said, waving the book.

"Wil is getting us together for something," I commented.

She gave me a cryptic smile as though she already knew what it was but wasn't going to give it away.

As we approached, I noticed Coleman walking up as well, but he didn't look at us. I got the distinct feeling that he, like myself, was thinking deeply about our shared experience. By the time we reached the fire circle, it was almost dark, and everyone was there: Rachel and I were located on one side of the fire, with Adjar, Hira, and Coleman on the other side.

Wil was standing apart, as though he was going to address us, and Wolf positioned himself at one side of the fire, holding a long pole he'd been using to stoke the blaze. Grandmother was behind all of us, directly under the cottonwood, making extremely slow dancing moves with her feet. Tommy was by her side.

At this moment, Wolf took his stick and spread the fire out into a wider area, killing most of the flames and sending a whirlwind of tiny sparks into the air. Then Wil asked us to sit down in a circle across from each other on the six small logs surrounding the glowing coals.

Rachel tossed me a glance and made her way over to sit down opposite Coleman. And as it happened, Hira and Adjar sat directly across from each other. Too late, I realized I was the odd man out. I was about to comment when, to my surprise, Tommy walked up, and with a maturity beyond his years raised his eyebrows as if to ask my permission to sit across from me.

"Of course," I said.

For a long time, we just all looked at one another, the hot coals casting a red hue over our faces. It was completely dark now, and even though we were all less than twelve feet from the person across from us, in the low light it was hard to bring each other's faces into focus. It was almost as though we were being forced to just look at the person as a whole shape, with few cues from body language or facial expression to guide our reactions. Setting up the fire this way, I thought, must be a Hopi psychological device.

"I wanted to get you all together," Wil began, "because Wolf was able to find the Sixth Integration. I also know many of you have made arrangements to leave, so I wanted to talk to you before you did so.

"The Document says that once one has experienced the Breakthrough to a God Connection, then one has completed the Foundation of Spirituality, a plateau of stable consciousness from which we can proceed, if we want to, with the remaining Integrations—a journey it calls a Rise to Sacred Influence.

"The Document describes this rise as a systematic recapturing of the full Divine Connection, piece by piece, as we elevate our consciousness back to that higher state. It culminates with the discovery of the Twelfth level, and at this point we will be able to maintain this consciousness."

Wil paused here and looked out at us.

"However," he continued, "it says, very clearly, that all those around you during a time of Breakthrough are there for an important reason. They represent a group that can help you move more rapidly through the remaining Integrations. And according to the Document, they have another important purpose as well: together you can form what it calls a Template of Agreement, which serves the role of agreeing on the truth about each Integration and influencing others with the power of that agreement.

"These template groups are very important because, to the extent that they are made up of people representing different religious traditions, they act to counteract and resolve the dangerous polarization and hatred growing between religious extremists in the world."

Wil walked closer to us. "The templates have such an effect on the extremists because, as we proceed through the remaining Integrations and grow in influence, we will be beaming one central truth

out to the world: that, in their essence, the religions are all pointing to the same experience of God Connection that most of us have
now shared. It is this common experience, once recognized, that can
serve to help reconcile the differences between religions and help
them come to unity. Truth, remember, is contagious."

I couldn't see their expressions entirely, but I could feel the gri-
maces on Adjar's and Hira's faces, and maybe even Coleman's. The
last thing many of us seemed to want, going into this gathering, was
to hang around long enough to make it through today, much less
long enough for some kind of unification to take place.

Wil was pausing again, knowing he had just dropped a bomb-
shell on everyone. I looked over toward Wolf and swore I could feel
him wink.

"Before you make your decisions in this regard," Wil went on, "I
want to tell you what the Document says is at stake. As with earlier
Integrations, enough people in the world must take these remaining
steps in order for the Influence to become powerful enough to counteract the dangers that are rapidly growing out there. To not act is to
send out another kind of contagion, one of giving up on the world."

That did it, I thought. Now all of us were in the same bind. We
might want to flee and save ourselves, but if we did, the continued
polarization might bring the world to destruction. In reality, the situation had been the same since the First Integration. None of us had
any choice at all.

As we looked at one another in silence, I noticed Hira was fidgeting
in her seat, as though she knew something that we didn't.

Finally, she shouted, "If this is all true, what are we doing just
talking about it? Let's get going with this! They're still out there. We
need to figure all this out!"

She looked at Rachel. "The whole time I heard you and Adjar discussing the Documents and experiencing the elevations, I experienced them with you. But I didn't tell you something important and neither did Adjar. Anish and the rest of these people already have a plan to destroy the world. And they're going to do it!"

She looked directly at Adjar. "You know what I'm saying is true! Tell them!"

Adjar got up and looked away, and for a moment, I thought he was going to just walk into the darkness. Instead, he looked back at us and slowly sat down.

"That's right," he said. "They have a plan to force the end of time. The group we were with is composed of two extreme factions, one looking to the Muslim tradition of Allah, and those following the Western religions of God or Jehovah. Both factions believe that before the end times can come, certain historical events, outlined in scriptural Prophecy, must first take place.

"Each side also believes that when these events occur, their respective holy men will return to gather up the true believers, vanquish their enemies, and set up a completely spiritual world on Earth based on their particular doctrine.

"But their dominant belief is that it is their duty to bring about these prophetic events as soon as possible. They have suspended their hatred in order to cooperate with one another, at least for a while. They call themselves Apocalyptics, and they have one stated goal: to bring about this last war that will make all this happen—Armageddon."

I couldn't believe what I was hearing. Adjar was describing the same threat that Peterson had warned of, only this was worse: a coalition of Western and Arabic groups who were actively working *together* to end the world.

It all made sense now, the fact that the group had both Arabic and Western members, and that they were arguing among themselves so much. They had formed an uneasy truce to go out and start the last war, after which they would just let the best religion win, so to speak, with each side thinking their tradition would be the one to prevail.

As he talked, I could feel Adjar softening. He, too, knew none of us had a choice. If there was a way to gain some kind of influence over people stuck in this kind of ideology, who were capable of doing such incredible damage, we had to at least try.

"I once believed," Adjar continued, "that this world was doomed, and I, too, wished for the coming of the Divine so as to bring about an ideal world to replace it. So I joined the Apocalyptics. But this group has now decided to use all violence necessary to protect their plan and provoke a total war, and that is why I had to leave them. When I escaped from them, I also experienced a Breakthrough that changed everything for me."

He looked openly at Hira for the first time, and I could sense her recalling more of her Breakthrough experience as well.

"It is the same with me," she said. "The coming of the Divine must happen. And humans must help somehow. But the end times should not be pushed to occur through violence. I had to reject the way of the Apocalyptics as well."

Suddenly, I remembered something. For some reason, the talk about God intervening to save the world brought back the mysterious point of Connection I had experienced on Secret Mountain. The memory flooded back into my mind. During the inflow of love and euphoria, I had experienced a point, or source, from which the love seemed to be flowing. I had even experienced a flash of knowing that the end times Prophecies had another meaning, not yet understood.

"The Document says," Wil offered, "that a template group can't go forward unless all the members realize it is their true mission to be involved."

There was silence as we looked at one another, or, as was the case in the low light, at one another's forms—and maybe at one another's spirits. Slowly, I realized we were all beginning to come together again. I could feel it in the exact same way I could feel it on Secret Mountain. And Tommy and Adjar were natural additions.

I looked over at Wolf. Were these Hopis so smart they knew how to help move us back toward Connection...with a fire?

What ensued was a round of mutual self-revealing, where each of us described how our spiritual journey had brought us to this moment, and to our preferred religious tradition. Adjar told us he was schooled as a Muslim and in the past few years had become interested in the Prophecy of the Islamic Messiah figure, the Twelfth Imam. And Hira, who had lived all her life in Israel, said she was most interested in the Jewish utopia that would be created after the arrival of their expected Messiah.

Then came Rachel, who said she was Christian in her belief, but she had studied end times prophecies as well, especially the Rapture—the idea that all believers would be lifted up in a spiritual body and protected from Armageddon. She found it meaningful that most traditions have some ideal of a Rapture-like event in their own Prophecies.

Tommy spoke up next, looking slightly nervous. He glanced at Grandmother and then said he represented the Native peoples' tradition, as he had studied the Mayan Prophecy and grew up with both Hopi and Yaqui influences. During his vision quest last year, he, too, had been given a Breakthrough experience. Now he was most fascinated by the Mayan Calendar. This Calendar could also be described, he told us, as itself an end-times prophecy, because it called for an end of a stage in creation and the beginning of something more ideal.

"According to the Maya," he said, "we will enter a time when enlightenment is more readily available, but it will not be imposed. We must realize that the quest shared by all those alive today is to access the unknown part of ourselves from which this consciousness springs."

I couldn't believe my ears. I, like so many others, had intuited that the Calendar was pointing to something new in history. And here was a young man professing to understand it who was saying the same thing. As he talked, I began to feel that understanding the Calendar would be a big part of the coming Integrations, especially the Twelfth.

With Tommy, all the major traditions were covered, except for Eastern religions. Everyone looked around.

"I've always leaned toward the Eastern path," Wil abruptly said. He then gave us a clear summary of his life, one of a driven search for a practical understanding of spiritual consciousness.

Now there was silence again as all eyes moved to Coleman. He told us generally about his life and his movement from spiritual skeptic to explorer of our deeper nature. But when it came to religion, he just shrugged his shoulders. Everyone seemed to accept that, but I still felt he was thinking about something he didn't want to mention yet.

When I focused again on the group, I could feel all eyes were on me.

"I love parts of all of the religions," I blurted.

Wil laughed, but the others were quiet at first, and then they began chuckling, too, until we were all laughing out loud. In that moment we came together even more. We were moving toward that peak Connection we had experienced on the mountain—with almost the same ease of interaction and speaking.

"The Document states," Wil finally added, "that once the members of a group experience the reality of a Divine Connection, they understand that it is the same for everyone, regardless of religious background. And they can see one other thing as well: that each religion in the world emphasizes only a few aspects of this experience. Other elements are minimized, and still others are left out altogether.

"Think about what this means!" he continued. "Among all the religions, the experience is adequately covered. But taken alone, each religion is incomplete. Therefore, what is needed is for each religion to teach what it has correct about Divine Connection to all the others, and then learn from the others what is missing in its own teachings.

"This is the only way the whole experience can be understood and ultimately made part of humanity's everyday reality. This is the purpose of the template groups—to reach a consensus concerning this natural reconciliation of the religions, for all to see.

"And remember, there are many groups of this kind coming together out there. Some will have it more right than others. But over time, through Conscious Conversation, the most truthful reconciliations will evolve in the public mind and become more powerful in their influence on human culture as we all move through the remaining Integrations."

We were all following him completely, maintaining and even building on the energy level. Now we were no longer just members of various religions. We were a group of souls who had decided to help make history.

When I awakened the next morning, my head was still buzzing from the experience of the night before—especially the revelation that the extremist group already had a plan to start Armageddon. How many template groups, I wondered, would it take to reach these Apocalyptics and others like them? A thousand? Ten thousand?

As I pushed my way out of the tent, I saw that the others were already drinking coffee and watching a colorful dawn dance across a dark blue sky. I walked toward them, and when Coleman saw me, he dashed over, holding several pages of the Document.

"There's something else in the Sixth Integration," he said, pointing toward a particular passage. "Right here it says another tradition should be part of the reconciliation of religion as well—one that would engage in exploring spirituality through a lens that strives to be as objective as possible."

"Whom are you talking about?" I asked sleepily.

"Us scientists!" he replied. "I can bring the viewpoint of the scientific tradition to our template group!"

Many of the others had heard what he said and all, including Wil, were nodding their heads in agreement. Coleman looked at me.

"Yeah," I said, "of course."

By midmorning, we had eaten breakfast and headed back to the circle again. Wolf had rebuilt the fire, but smaller now, just enough to break the morning chill.

For a long time, we stared at one another, embracing the feeling we'd reached the night before. Then Wil began.

"The Document discusses," he said, "a few basic agreements that have to be reached before a template group can move forward, agreements that are key for this process to be effective. One is this: in no way should we think that the adherents of any one tradition should have to give up belief in the validity of their chosen way— only that they must seek to integrate the best of the rest.

"And the other agreement is that no one should think of their path as the only way to Divine Connection. Remember, we all experienced this Breakthrough despite the different religious perspectives we brought with us. The Connection occurred because we were in the same place of willingness and need to open up to a greater Divine Consciousness."

What Wil had expressed was undeniable fact; we *had* all experienced the same breakthrough, and it meant that there were many paths, but only one direct experience. For a long moment, we all looked at one another again, the anticipation palpable. Then Wil smiled and looked down at the Document.

"It says to begin," he stated, "with a focus on the element of the God Experience that has most remained in memory."

We all just waited to see who would speak first. Then everyone's eyes seem to fall on Coleman.

"As a scientist," Coleman finally said, "the first element for me of this Connection was a sense of overriding well-being and love, the feeling of having rejoined a lost part of myself, and of being cared for and protected."

Everyone was nodding in agreement.

"How, then," Wil said, "would the rest of you describe this love and belonging element of the God Connection?"

"The Holy Spirit filled us," Rachel replied.

"Allah gave us his guidance," Adjar commented.

"God rewarded our work," said Hira.

Everyone looked at Tommy.

"Spirit filled the world and it came alive!" he said with a power that surprised everyone.

Coleman seemed to be thinking again. "Wait a minute. Those are religious descriptions. We need to speak more precisely about the actual experience of coming home to love, and discern which tradition emphasizes this the most."

Rachel was about ready to burst.

"There is only one tradition," she said, "that especially emphasizes Divine Love: Christianity. I know that the word *love* often sounds hollow, and we fall short in always expressing love. But we do believe that, if we humbly seek this experience, we can move into and feel what we felt on the mountain. We are lifted above our old lives, and all the mistakes we've made are transcended. We are made new and more whole.

"To me, this experience felt like coming home, where we are finally free from all those things we wish we hadn't done. There's a sense that when we reach this Connection, we can start over."

No one spoke. We all knew she was right. The love and well-being we felt did feel like leaving the past behind.

"We teach that anyone," she continued, "who wants to come home and start over can find that experience. But it means refuting the idea of an eye for an eye. As we saw on Secret Mountain, at a higher consciousness, there's no justification for a Cycle of Revenge, no possibility of it. The truth is that we have to allow everyone to have the ability to change, to be redeemed in the blink of an eye."

I couldn't believe she was addressing the Cycle of Revenge. Colonel Peterson had said it couldn't be overcome. Was there another tradition that refuted the Cycle of Revenge, even if they couldn't live up to it?

Finally, Adjar spoke. "I must admit that our tradition does not emphasize this element of love and forgiveness, not the way we experienced it. And our tradition too often does hold on to revenge and punishment as basic principles. In fact, I never understood forgiveness until our Breakthrough. But we do have parts of our tradition, such as the Sufis, who say essentially the same thing—they just do not receive much attention."

Several other people then commented on the little-known scriptures found within their traditions that likewise pointed to the same idea of love and transcending the past.

"So," Wil said, "do we agree that Christianity has the best emphasis on this element of the God Experience? An emphasis that the others, to be accurate in describing this experience, should integrate as well?"

Tommy spoke up. "Native peoples have sometimes been

focused on revenge and enemies. I agree that Christianity has the most emphasis."

"I agree as well," Wil said. "Eastern thought speaks more in terms of bliss, but also has currents of teaching about love and reconciliation. But transformational love, in the Christian tradition, is the most accurate."

Everyone else was nodding in agreement.

"Okay," Wil continued. "But I have to raise a question we touched on earlier. Rachel, I'll start with you. Can you acknowledge that people from other religions can reach this euphoric place from within their own tradition?"

She looked at him with total honesty. "I have to admit I have always had a problem accepting that, primarily because of our scripture's injunction that no one comes to God except through Christ. And I know others here have the same exclusive feeling about their own paths."

I looked around, sensing we had reached a roadblock. The main challenge to religious reconciliation had been put squarely on the table before us.

Then an idea came to me, and without thinking I said, "But Rachel, you do believe that, at baptism, Christ reunited completely with God, right? And became equal with God in the doctrine of the Trinity?"

She nodded.

"Wouldn't it make sense that if someone was sincerely searching for Divine Connection and really found it, even if they never knew of Christ, they would have passed along the same path of expanding consciousness that Christ demonstrated? And so would have gone through Christ in a way? Maybe that's what the scriptures actually mean."

The group seemed stunned at my remark, and they all looked at Rachel.

She looked at me for a long moment, then smiled. "Yes, I now think so, because after our experience, I think that Connecting is a matter of letting go and opening up to a greater consciousness. Therefore, I think you are correct, although it is belief and affirmation that gets us started."

Now Rachel's gaze centered on Hira, as if to ask, Will you grant that your way is not the only way? That all other traditions can find love and redemption?

"This whole discussion shakes me," Hira said, returning her look. "Like all of you, I experienced an inner security and sense of being loved and cared for, in spite of every shortcoming. So I would have to say, in light of direct experience, my tradition must acknowledge that instant redemption can take place, and that people of other faiths can move into Connection with the one God."

She smiled, adding: "And the fact is, we have our own scriptures and prophets that have said much the same thing."

She stopped and glanced at Adjar, who was looking back at her in complete acceptance. We could all feel a thick wall, built during centuries of conflict, beginning to melt away.

"I know your people have suffered, too," Adjar said. "And I can give you your path. There is only one Divine Connection, and it is the same for us all no matter what path we choose, as long as it is loving and genuine."

For several minutes, we just looked at one another and felt the rising love and Connection.

Finally, Wil said, "Now there is another element that we have remembered: the sense of personal and collective mission that we felt during our Breakthrough, an experience that led us to form this group. Which tradition most emphasizes the knowingness that we are here on Earth to do something important?"

Immediately, Hira spoke up. "You're talking about the Judaic tradition. We believe that to be in God's Connection is to be given a work to do. The Connection with the Divine doesn't give us just love and forgiveness. It also gives us a mission that we know in our hearts has to be done. I don't know about the rest of you, but on the mountain, I experienced the certain knowledge that there is a plan, and each of us is a part of it."

Everyone nodded, and several people noted that their traditions also had strong scriptures that gave importance to mission. They just weren't emphasized enough.

"So we agree," Wil asked, "that the Judaic tradition is best at emphasizing the part of the Connection that is a realization of mission?"

I could tell that the clarity about mission—reinforced as it was with our decision to create a Template of Agreement—was elevating our consciousness even more. We had now recaptured three elements of our Divine Connection: love and all that comes with it, Protection and redemption. And now mission. I could see the elevation on every face.

"All we had to do," Wil said, "in order to hold the Fifth and Sixth Integrations was to remember how these elements felt and to seek to come back to them if they were lost. If we lose this Connection of love, for instance, it's because it has been replaced by one of the lower emotions. Seek to return to love, the primary emotion of Connection, and these other emotions will drop away. Then, once in love, Protection and mission come to us as well. The key going forward is to *listen*."

Wil put a special emphasis on the word *listen*, and I knew it was his way of hinting at the next Integration.

"Do you know anything about the Seventh Integration?" I asked.

Wil gave us a knowing look.

"We haven't found that part of the Document yet," Wil said, "but I'd bet the Seventh is about discovering more of the Law of Connection. We have to find our full powers of intuition and realize it is how we are guided."

THE ART OF TUNING IN

As the sun began to sink in the west, I suddenly felt the urge to walk down the hill past the pond to the rocky area that had earlier attracted me for some reason. Wil had ended our last session very abruptly—so quickly, in fact, that I had the eerie sense we might be leaving soon, and I wanted to see this part of the homestead while I still had the chance.

As I walked, more thoughts about the Seventh Integration came to mind. The old Prophecy had predicted that, at some point, humanity would heighten its perception of those inner impressions long classified as intuitions, hunches, and so-called gut feelings. After years of emphasizing rational thought and logic during the dominance of the material and secular worldview, it predicted we would finally take seriously the treasure of information coming from the right hemisphere of the brain: the part that gave us a sense of knowing, without being aware exactly of how we knew.

At this moment, I caught sight of a lone figure walking about two hundred yards to the left of me. It was Tommy, walking back toward the homestead. For an instant, I thought about turning around or yelling out to him, because I wanted to know more about the Mayan Calendar. Yet for some reason I kept walking, certain now that I

121

came down here for a reason. I felt sure a Synchronicity was about to happen.

After several minutes, I entered a sandy area dotted with prickly pear cacti next to a grove of large mesquite trees. Without warning, a man suddenly walked out of the mesquite. Peterson!

I grimaced. This wasn't what I was expecting.

"I need to talk to you," he said. "It's serious."

He glanced up toward the house to make sure no one else was coming, and he urged me to follow him farther into the grove.

"Do you know those extremists are still looking for you?" he said.

"We were hoping they'd left," I replied.

"Some of them did, but they left a few to search for you. Do you know who these people are?"

I nodded.

He was shaking his head, worried. "It took us awhile to piece together what they're trying to do. It's exactly what I was talking about. They're raising the stakes."

"What are you going to do about them?" I asked.

He looked away. "I don't know. What are you learning from this Document?"

I thought for a moment about whether to answer, then decided to just tell the truth. "The Document is describing a way to stop the escalation of violence."

"The templates," he said.

I was startled. "So you're actually reading this thing."

"It's my job."

"But do you understand what you're reading? Did you see we were protected?"

He chuckled. "I saw you were lucky. If we hadn't come along, you wouldn't have made it."

"I don't think it was luck," I said.

"It doesn't matter," he pressed. "Listen to me. Things are accelerating, just like I said they would. Even with the action that's been taken with Iran, nothing has changed. Iran is still working on nukes. We think they may already have the capability to give them to terrorists."

I looked at him hard. "I heard the Apocalyptics already have a plan to create a war."

He straightened his sunglasses. "I'm still hoping this crazy Document might give us another way out. As I told you, no one is going to like what we'll have to do to stop this threat."

In that moment, I realized that contacting us and following the progress of the Document was something he was doing much more on his own than I had thought. And as we exchanged looks, I could also tell he knew I knew.

"I'm way out on a limb here," he said. "And we're both running out of time."

He looked at me as though asking for more information. So I began to describe as best I could what the Breakthrough on the mountain felt like, and the idea that the Templates of Understanding could somehow create a wave of influence that might dispel the Apocalyptics' intentions, although we didn't fully understand how to do it yet.

He shook his head, looking at me as though all was lost.

"That's what this Document is talking about, some crazy idea like that?"

I knew how he felt. From the perspective of the secular worldview, it *would* seem illogical and silly. There was no way one could just read the words of the Document and understand, unless one had also encountered the experiences it was describing.

"Listen," I said, "I know it sounds crazy to you, but there's an esoteric connection between people. It's a real influence. If this catches on, it could work."

"Well," he said, shaking his head, "keep looking. And you'd better do it quickly. I told you: measures are being taken domestically in every Western-leaning country to deal with this problem. And if the plans go forward, it will happen before anyone realizes it's under way."

"Wait a minute," I said. "You act like you can just take over nations that have a long tradition of democracy."

He looked away. "Unfortunately, it's not that hard, especially during difficult economic times. Look at Venezuela. All you have to do is get a majority of the population hooked on government subsidies, and then threaten to take them away. They'll vote for the people who promise to take care of them, especially if you co-opt the world's largest corporations at the same time and get them to buy media companies.

"You just have to make both Left and Right think you're doing it to support their ideology, then everyone looks the other way while you hide the power to do it in bills nobody reads, and gradually plant your own judges in key places. Once you nationalize the polling booths, the rest is easy. You just wait for the right time, the right emergency."

His certainty at being able to pull off such a ploy chilled me. He seemed to realize he'd said too much and quickly reached into a satchel and pulled out a large folder.

"These are copies of the Seventh Integration," he said, moving to leave.

I reached out and took the folder. "Where are you getting these copies?"

"This one was sent to the office of the CIA in Langley. Do you believe that? If you were releasing parts of a document like this, would you send one to them? I managed to get them forwarded to me through a friend before anyone upstairs noticed, then ran a full investigation. It went nowhere. We don't have a clue who's distributing these translations."

He headed farther into the bushes. "You have five more days to give me some information I can use."

I hurried back to the house where I found Coleman, Adjar, and Hira gathered around Wil, already sensing something was wrong. Rushing up to them I rapidly relayed what Peterson had said, including that the extremists were still here, looking for us.

"I think," Wil said, "that we need to leave as soon as we can."

Adjar leaned in. "And go where? How will we know how to proceed until we find the Seventh Integration?"

I lifted up the folder I had tucked under my arm, which surprised everyone.

They grinned at me as if I had produced a miracle, and then each took a copy to read.

"Where's Tommy?" I asked Wil, still thinking the Mayan Calendar would shed more light on all this.

"His mother sent a friend to bring him to her. She's in Egypt."

"What? Why? Isn't it dangerous there?"

"I know the person she sent," Wil said. "He's reliable. He said Tommy was needed."

I stood up, feeling angry.

Wil walked closer. "Look, Tommy is not an ordinary child. There's another template group there that his mother is part of. Tommy's been there with her many times before. He'll be fine."

I nodded. "Where's Rachel?"

"She went with them."

I just looked at him, dumbfounded and slightly disoriented. Things were moving too fast.

"Why would she do that?" I asked.

"She felt that she had to. And there was no time to wait to say good-bye."

I wondered again why I hadn't turned around and come back when I had seen Tommy. Yet if I had, I may not have seen Peterson and received the copies of the Seventh Integration. I knew all this was just more Synchronicity, moving us along, but I didn't like it.

Wil was looking at the pages.

"Let's get going," he said. "We have to read this!"

I nodded, sat down by my tent, and began reading. The Document opened by saying that, in this Integration, we would see how Synchronicity actually worked.

Moments of Synchronistic discovery, it went on, feel like we are in just the right place at just the right time to receive important information. Yet if we observe more closely, we can see that these Synchronistic moments are preceded by an intuitive urge that directs us to go somewhere, or say something, that results in the Synchronicity. Following such guidance has happened all through history at moments of great discovery and accomplishment. But it has happened more or less unconsciously.

It is time, the Document continued, to wake up and bring the intuitive part of Synchronicity more fully into consciousness. The key to doing this is to broaden our habit of expecting Synchronicity to include expecting the intuitions that are part of this process. And in order to do that, we must adequately identify such guidance by learning to distinguish our "guiding" thoughts from ordinary "ego strategy" thoughts.

I looked over at Wil. "This is similar to what was said in the Prophecy at the Seventh Insight."

"Read a little further," Wil replied. "It explains how to actually do it."

Ego thoughts, the Document clarified, are words we say to ourselves about our situation in order to logically assess how to get things done in the world. These thoughts come up spontaneously from years of learning.

However, the Document says that if we observe closely, we can begin to distinguish another kind of thought, one that appears to be more spontaneous. It feels as if it merely drops into our minds, usually without any direct connection to logical analysis. These thoughts often come with an image of us doing something, or a feeling that urges us to take some action that we feel in our stomachs. These are thoughts the document is calling guidance. Once followed, they usually lead to an important Synchronicity.

I thought about this for a moment. That *is* exactly how it happens. How many times when we suddenly think to call an old friend, for instance, does the person say, "I was just thinking about you," and then present a Synchronicity of some kind?

I looked at Wil, who pretended not to notice but gave me the hint of a frown. I knew what he was saying to me: don't talk, hurry up and read.

The rest of the pages wrapped up the Integration by saying, again, that the key to becoming fully conscious of these thoughts is to stay as much as possible in this state of alertness for the next guiding intuition to arrive. The key was to not let a hunch or an image go by without at least seriously considering it. It did reiterate, as before, that since we were in a transition, adding spiritual ability to a rational, logic-oriented worldview, we should use logic first in finding a way to act on the intuition.

One tip for being on the alert for a guidance was to constantly ask yourself, "Why did I think that now?"

I put down the papers, realizing I already asked that question of myself from time to time. How did I get into that habit? Then I remembered: Wil had told me to do it while we were in Peru.

As I read on, the Document mentioned another technique to use when one needs a guiding intuition, or higher perspective, on a given situation in a hurry. Instead of just waiting, one can actively seek guidance by "tuning in."

For instance, when facing a decision whether to go somewhere or not, we can just imagine ourselves already traveling to the place and arriving there. The point of this method is to see how easily the journey can be visualized. If you can see yourself going there easily, then that means it's a good idea. If the desired images are difficult to see, or fail to appear altogether, we should take precautionary measures.

The Document reiterated that when we see the right course of action, there is a corresponding elevation in energy, or an "urging" feeling, as though one is "inspired" to take the action.

I stopped and thought about this process for a moment. *Tuning in* was already part of the worldwide vocabulary. What the Document seemed to be relaying is that there is a more precise way this art should be practiced.

Returning to the Document, I saw that it made one last point. It said we could use this method to tune in to many different life situations, but we would not discover how deeply we could tune in, until enough people returned to the Mount.

The statement threw me into deep thought. Was that meant to be taken literally or was it symbolic? And if it was literal, what Mount? There were dozens of mountains mentioned in the sacred writings of the world. Looking over at Wil, I saw he had placed his pages on his lap and was gazing into the distance. Hira and Adjar were doing the same thing nearby. When I caught sight of Coleman, he was slowly strolling down toward the big cottonwood, also appearing to be deep in thought. I immediately knew what they were doing: they were pondering our current situation and looking for guidance. They were already tuning in.

Clearing my mind, I attempted to do the same thing, first seeing if anything just popped into my mind. For a long time I simply
looked around the area, letting my mind drift. I mused about how
nice this homestead felt, and how sad I would be to leave it. Then
I thought about our group's joint experiences on Secret Mountain,
and whether the Mount the Document mentioned might be that
mountain.

Suddenly, I got the image of another place, a hazy, very rocky,
mountainous region. And I was there with Rachel! Which gave me a
blast of energy. Barely able to contain my excitement, I looked at Wil
again, who seemed to be waiting for me to finish.

He stood up and came over to me. I caught sight of Coleman
walking my way as well. Hira and Adjar were right behind him.
Soon we were all standing in a circle facing one another.

"I know what I need to do," Wil said. "We still have no idea
where the Twelfth part of this Document has been released, if anywhere. Sooner or later we're going to have to find it. I'm going to my
friend's place in Cairo to see if I can discover a clue."

Adjar stepped forward. "I'm going back home to Saudi Arabia.
There's another mountain there that has something to do with all
this."

All eyes then fell on me.

"I saw myself with Rachel," I said. "Where was she going?"

Wil gave me a big smile. "She went to the city of St. Katherine,
Egypt, near *Mount* Sinai!"

I just looked at him as the others laughed. The energy was soaring. The Document said we all had to return to the Mount. Maybe
we were all going to different ones.

"What about you?" I asked Coleman. "Where are you going?"

"I'm going with *you*," he replied.

"Are you sure?"

"Look, all this is new to me. I'm the one who went the wrong way when the extremists were shooting at us from the ridge, remember? I tried to discern what to do, and all I saw was myself with you, on another really rocky mountain of some kind." He smiled and winked.

I looked over at Wil, amazed at how much our energy was elevating.

"Do you feel this?" I asked. "We're getting the Seventh Integration, aren't we?"

He shot me a look. "Yeah, and we've felt it before!"

We looked at one another. Of course. We were recapturing this part of our Connection on Secret Mountain. We were stuck in this world all alone. We were guided. The full memory came back to me: the way I spontaneously knew what I was being led to do, the exact moves to make.

Hira stepped forward.

"Remember the template," she said. "We also have to come to agreement about guidance. Obeying God is talked about a lot in our tradition."

"Also in the Christian tradition," I said, feeling as though I was speaking for Rachel. "It's called doing God's will."

Wil was nodding. "In Eastern thought, it's best expressed in Zen, as a flow in harmony with the Divine."

"Yes," Adjar said. "But no tradition points to this ability more than my tradition. We call it surrendering to God. It is the foundation of our whole religion. The ego must be put in its proper place by the daily seeking of guidance in prayer, many times daily, so that we act only in spirit!"

He was right, and we all knew it. Islam did have the strongest emphasis on this part of our Connection.

"By the way," Hira said, "I'm going back to Jerusalem. I can't explain it, but something is happening at the Temple Mount, the place where the ruins of David's temple are located."

I felt a shiver. I knew somehow that her intuition was directly connected, in a way we didn't yet understand, to the Apocalyptics, and to their clandestine plan to end the world.

For an hour I helped everyone get ready to leave. Wil had managed to find a charter out of Sedona airport to Phoenix, then a flight to New York and Cairo. Adjar and Hira were driving to Phoenix and then flying to their respective destinations. Coleman and I had decided to stay the night and then leave early the next morning, primarily because we needed all day to take care of our cars and make arrangements.

Wolf had somehow secured clean cell phones for all of us, and at one point Wil handed them out.

"These will help us stay connected," Wil had said. "But remember, text only, no voice. Here is a list of everyone's numbers. Commit them to memory and then destroy the list. Everyone has a phone now except Rachel and Tommy. Just use the phone sparingly."

I followed Wil and helped take down his tent, uneasy that he was leaving again.

"What do you think is going to happen?" I asked.

He looked me up and down. "I think we're beginning a downhill run now. We're going to move through the rest of these Integrations and find the Twelfth. I just hope a lot of other people are doing the same thing out there. No matter what happens, just keep going. I'll find you at Sinai."

Within a couple of minutes he was loaded up and driving off with Hira, Adjar, and Wolf, giving me one last resolute wave.

"He has a great guide," Grandmother suddenly said from behind me.

I turned to find her standing several yards away, reaching out with a cup of tea smelling of sage and rosemary.

"This will help you on your path," she said.

"Grandmother," I replied, reaching for the tea, "you helped us get started with your dance."

She didn't answer but nodded out toward the distant horizon. I followed her eyes to see a larger sliver of moon hovering in the late afternoon sky.

Just then a crow cawed loudly down by the big tree, which made me flinch for some reason.

"You have a good guide, too," she said. "You will enjoy your visit to Sister Mountain."

She was still looking into the distance.

"Are you talking about Mount Sinai?" I asked.

She was walking away. "It is red, too, like the hills of Sedona."

"You live in an interesting world, Grandmother," I called out.

She stopped walking for an instant, not looking back, then smiled and continued on her way.

I was leaning back against a small tree near my tent wondering why Grandmother called Mount Sinai "Sister Mountain," when Coleman walked up.

"I wondered where you got off to," I said.

"I just took a walk," he replied, smiling. "I needed some time to reflect on everything you've gotten me into on this trip. I never dreamed I'd have these experiences, much less have to keep a scientific perspective on it all."

I nodded. "No kidding. A lot has happened. It's forcing us to put our spirituality into practice, and it's all been building on itself."

Coleman nodded as though he wanted me to elaborate, so I just let it come intuitively.

"The First Integration," I said, "sustaining Synchronistic flow, got us going. That's what was so hard to do before. All we have to do is expect it, and it happens. After that it's a matter of staying in that 'star of your own movie' centeredness by telling others the truth about your path and how it is unfolding. That's when each Synchronicity begins to lead to another one.

"Then we were shown how the Second Integration works. And how we should try to find a higher truth with others, even in uncomfortable encounters."

I nodded toward him, remembering our first conversation in which I'd written him off as a skeptic. He knew what I was thinking and laughed out loud.

"We were being shown," I went on, "that if we participate in Conscious Conversation, we can always receive a larger truth about how spirituality works. And thus we contribute to the building of an ever more complete, spiritual worldview.

"The Third Integration gave us an even larger picture of what happens when we stay in this centered truth, showing us that if we operate in truth, we fall into Alignment with the Law of Truth and can see the other laws that support this flow: Connection, Karma, and Service.

"If we hold to our truth as it evolves with others, and never lie or manipulate but strive to be of service, then we fall in harmony with the Law of Karma, avoiding its corrections, and naturally attract those who are there to be of service to us, so that we rapidly flow forward into a higher Connection with each other and the Divine.

"The Fourth Integration showed us the stakes involved in our quest to reach this deeper spiritual Connection. Those stuck in secular obsession are building ever more polarized systems of untruth and becoming more extreme in their dehumanization of each other, endangering everything.

"Thankfully, the Fifth and Sixth showed us a glimpse of how deep our Connection with the Divine could become, where we find love and, most important, Protection, and an awareness of mission. We realized we have a part in helping one another move through the rest of the Integrations. Now we have to figure out how to Rise to Influence and create this Template of Agreement that, supposedly, will reach those in fear."

I took a breath. "Which brings us to the present. The Seventh Integration showed us how to step up the Synchronicity even more by following the guidance that comes to us if we tune in."

I paused and looked at him, somewhat surprised that I had been able to voice the Integrations so quickly.

"You were right," Coleman said. "It's all a consciousness that builds on itself."

I looked at him a moment, then said, "It reminds me of a verse I learned as a child. Something like, 'If you are honorable over little you are given much.' I guess it turned out to be true."

"So what do you think is going to happen now?" Coleman asked.

"Hopefully," I said, "Synchronicity will continue to lead us through the remaining steps, and we'll continue to integrate more of the Connection we reached on the mountain... until we remember it all. That's when, I guess, we'll reach our strongest influence."

For a long moment we were both lost in thought.

Finally, Coleman said, "I just wish I could understand one thing I glimpsed up there. It was like a Connection point with all that I was feeling."

"What? Are you kidding me?"

"No, I really felt something. It was elusive and seemed to come and go."

I jumped to my feet. "I experienced the same thing!"

He looked amazed.

"Yeah," I repeated, "almost exactly as you described it!"

*   *   *

The next morning we were up early and, by first light, heading back toward Sedona. Wolf had returned late the night before, just in time to grab a few hours of sleep and to help us load our gear. Now, as we rode along in the early light of dawn, he looked tired but was still full of mischief.

"I have a surprise," he said.

"What is it?" I asked. Coleman was smiling from the backseat.

"Don't ask," he said. "You'll get it later."

We tried to pry it out of him, but he wouldn't budge and eventually all of us fell into a lengthy silence. Then, as we entered the city limits, we were treated to a beautiful Sedona sunrise, and as usual, people were pulled over on the side of the road and standing on some of the hills, ushering in the day. I wondered if the sunrise was Wolf's surprise, but I could tell from his face that it wasn't.

The sunrise invigorated each of us. We were all completely centered and setting a tone of expectant waiting without even talking about it. And we were alert, not just for a Synchronicity, but for the guidance that preceded it.

Suddenly, Wolf pulled into a side street and stopped, a worried look on his face.

"There's something wrong," he said to me. "My friends who were keeping your car were supposed to meet us back at that gas station we passed. They weren't there."

Coleman and I looked at each other.

Wolf thought for a moment, then said, "I believe I should take you straight to the Phoenix airport, right now, as fast as we can get there."

"Wait a minute," Coleman said. "My car is at my hotel. I can't just leave it. And what about the rest of my clothes?"

As he spoke, I tried to visualize us driving directly to the airport, easily seeing us arriving there and boarding the plane. Then I tried to picture us going to get the cars instead, and immediately had difficulty. In fact, I couldn't picture us getting to Coleman's hotel at all.

"I agree with Wolf," I said. "I think we should go now."

Coleman seemed unconvinced, but not overridingly so.

"I guess it's okay," he said. "I can contact my friends later and make arrangements for the car at that time."

"I would be careful calling anyone for a while," Wolf said.

Coleman was staring at me. "You seemed very clear that going ahead was the right thing to do."

I told him exactly what I had seen.

He thought for a moment, looking away, then said, "Yeah, I get the same thing now. You know, it's a lot harder to follow your intuition when it means having to change plans."

"Yeah," I said.

"You know," Coleman added, "we're tuning in, following the Seventh Integration exactly. Too bad we don't have a copy of the next Integration."

I saw Wolf perk up.

"Oh," he said, tongue in cheek, "Wil and I stopped by a friend's place to get some food for his trip."

He was reaching under the seat, pulling out a folder.

"Surprise!" he quipped. "Our friend happened to have a copy of the Eighth Integration. Now, since you're so good at tuning in to your guidance, you can learn something else."

He handed the folder to Coleman. "You can learn to tune in to people."

THE ONENESS INTENTION

$\mathbf{A}$s we began the two-hour trip to the airport, I wondered how we were going to find Rachel and Tommy. Wil knew they were headed to the city of St. Katherine in Egypt. But just where they were staying there was unknown.

"It's a small town," Wil had said. "You'll find them. Just pay attention. Something will happen."

I knew he was probably right. From the intuitions Coleman and I had experienced, we were definitely headed to the correct place. Egypt could be dangerous at times, but the government was usually friendly toward tourists, especially those who might be interested in a pilgrimage to Mount Sinai.

Coleman had put down the Document, so I grabbed it and began to read. As Wolf had hinted, the Eighth Integration said we would be led into another level of Connection with others, a level that would heighten our understanding of Conscious Conversation.

This stuff is coming fast now, I thought. Maybe Wil was right in saying we were beginning the downhill run through the remaining Integrations.

I reminded myself that the Eighth Insight of the old Prophecy had predicted we would learn to uplift others in conversation by intending to connect with and uplift their higher self or soul. This uplifting was intended to lift the other person into a higher consciousness, where, along with getting more insight into his or her own life, the person would be more likely to provide Synchronistic information that we individually needed.

At the time, there was some confusion about the mechanics of this procedure, but most times merely the intention worked. The people being uplifted would suddenly become more alert and seemingly gain access to an unconscious part of themselves. They would often preface their remarks by saying, "I don't know why I'm telling you this," or "I've never thought of this before, but..." And then the information they presented would often be exactly what we needed to hear at the time.

I looked back at the pages in my hand and moved to the next passage. It seemed to be saying that this uplifting could now be expanded, in light of the other Integrations, by consciously merging minds with the higher self of the other person. Merging minds?

At this point, I was interrupted in my reading as we entered the northern outskirts of Phoenix and began our own search for food. After about thirty minutes, we found a health food store where we stocked up. And as fortune would have it, immediately next door was a small shop where Coleman could buy more clothes.

Afterward, we took a back way to the airport, where Wolf pulled up very cautiously to the international concourse. We were all on the lookout for anything unusual and tried to be hypervigilant for any intuitions meant to guide our way. However, nothing of note happened, so Coleman and I jumped out and collected our gear.

Finally, I walked over to the window and shook Wolf's hand and thanked him.

"Get to Sister Mountain as soon as you can," he said cryptically. "You'll be shown what to do."

In less than an hour, we were on an airplane headed for Cairo, taxiing out to the runway. I checked my cell phone and found no messages, then quickly shut it off as the plane lifted into the air.

Coleman was already asleep, so I pulled out the Eighth Integration and began reading again. It went on to explain the passage about merging minds by saying we could initiate this merging by applying what it called the "Oneness Intention."

This term, the Document went on, meant much more than the abstract idea, voiced by many religious traditions, that we are all one. It defined an entirely new way that humans could relate to one another, the effectiveness of which could immediately be proven to oneself. Further, the best way to understand this new way of relating was to look closely at the phenomenon of people finishing each other's sentences.

I thought about this for a moment. I'd always concluded that this ability resulted from how much time one spent with a particular person, primarily because it seemed so common among husbands and wives, executives and their secretaries, and roommates and office mates.

When I turned again to the Document, it said that while this ability is common, it could be more readily facilitated, even among strangers, by practicing the Oneness Principal, which was to go into every human interaction with the intention of joining higher minds.

Wait a minute, I thought, putting on the mental brakes. Would we really want to do that? I was suddenly feeling a real resistance to this idea. In fact, I was so perplexed by my reaction that I woke up Coleman and told him everything I'd read, and the trouble I was having with merging minds with others, especially strangers. Perhaps because the idea was planted, I couldn't help seeing him in a totally different light. In fact, he seemed to behave in a slightly different way, as though he was more thoughtful than before.

"As a guy with a strong ego myself," he said, "it comes to me that perhaps you don't like the idea of merging minds with other people because you're afraid they will pollute your thinking with gibberish."

I laughed, and then thought about what he was saying. Was that it? Did I just want to feel special and unique, and that led me to think merging minds with someone might dilute my creativity?

"On the other hand," he continued, "you can't deny that our group has been joined, in a way, already, and acting in unison. Remember how powerfully that was happening on Secret Mountain?"

I did remember. We were in that connected state for hours. And the fact was, I felt no diminishment or loss of energy from the Connection at all. If anything, I felt enhanced. We were somehow all coordinating our actions and decisions at light speed, like a flock of birds in flight do when they change directions at precisely the same time. And we experienced the same phenomenon at the homestead as well.

I looked at the Document again, and it clarified that the joining is not of egos but of the higher mind, which is linked with the Divine. To further explain, it said when two people merge in this manner, both feel enlarged because they have access to not just their own higher self, but to the other's higher consciousness as well. The net effect is to feel more clarity and guidance overall. The clarification made me feel better.

"Seems to me," Coleman continued, his eyelids looking heavy again, "that since it says you can prove the power of the Oneness Intention for yourself, you should just try it for a while." With that, he was suddenly asleep again.

Looking out the window, I mused over the succinctness of his suggestion. In fact, it sounded like something I might have said to myself, if he hadn't beaten me to it. Why not try it now? I thought. I quickly moved everything off my lap and walked up to the attendants' station to ask for some more water.

Only one of the attendants was there, an older Egyptian woman with short black hair, dressed in uniform, who had served us earlier. I decided to do just as the Document said. As I walked up, I silently affirmed the intention to join higher minds.

She immediately turned around. "Need a refill?"

"Yes, please," I replied, handing her my empty cup. "It's going to be a long flight, huh?"

"Yes, but it's not too bad. I crew this flight several times a week."

She was looking at my shoulder. "Is that for me?"

I looked down and realized that I still had the copy of the Document under my arm. I had placed it there when I was moving everything so I could get out of my seat, then forgot to put it back in my pack.

"Oh, no, it's just a copy of an old . . . well, just something I brought with me by mistake."

"An old what?"

She looked at me with total earnestness, and I realized I had to tell the truth about it.

"It's an old Document about human spirituality that people are studying right now."

"What's it about?"

I struggled to put it simply. "Well, it's about how humans are waking up to the fact that we're all spiritually connected."

She looked down as if thinking, then said: "I've heard something about this. My sister's husband is studying some writings like that. There's a whole group of them."

Leaning in and speaking lower, she added, "You know he usually is shy and reserved, but since he's been meeting with this group, he's really become quite talkative and obsessed with telling the truth."

"That's the same Document," I said, somewhat surprised by

the familiarity with which she was speaking to me, as if she was talking to her close friend. I couldn't wait for the answer to my next question.

"Where does your sister live?" I asked.

"In a small town out in the desert, called St. Katherine."

I had already known what she was going to say, but the Synchronicity still shocked me.

"You won't believe this," I said. "That's where we're going after Cairo."

Her eyes lit up. "Really? I should give you his number. His name is Joseph." She opened a drawer and pulled out some paper and scribbled down his complete name and telephone number.

"You know," she continued, "I haven't talked to him in quite a while. I'm going to call him and ask more about this Document. I'll tell him we met on a plane."

"Thanks," I said, then gave her my name and number as well.

The other attendant came up at this point, so I walked back to my seat and immediately woke up Coleman and told him what happened.

"You should be used to this kind of Synchronicity by now," he said.

"N-n-no," I stammered. "It usually doesn't go this fast with a stranger. A Synchronicity this on target usually takes quite a bit of time to come out in conversation, if it happens at all. Sometimes you feel led to someone, but when you try to talk, the conversation goes nowhere. Two strangers usually have to build up trust."

Suddenly wide awake, he looked at me hard. "You did what I said, didn't you? You tried that Oneness principle."

I gave him an exaggerated nod yes. Coleman pulled the copy of the Document out of my hand. "Let me read this for a while."

Which was fine with me. I wanted to spend some more time thinking. Maybe I was making too much out of the woman's openness, but I didn't think so. What struck me as important wasn't so much meeting a friendly person who had a brother-in-law in the city of our destination. That wasn't crazy unlikely. The noteworthy thing was the quality of the conversation itself: there was an immediate closeness and rapport and, in fact, honesty. At this level of Connection, I didn't have to remember to be direct and honest. My words just came out that way naturally.

When I woke up, Coleman was already awake and arranging his things. He leaned over when he saw me stirring.

"What time is it?" I asked.

"Two A.M.," he said. "We'll be landing in Cairo in twenty minutes."

He looked sleepy, as though the crowded seats had further fatigued him during the night. And I felt the same way. I couldn't have slept more than a few hours.

Once on the ground, we hurried to pick up our luggage and find our ride to St. Katherine. When it arrived, we were pleased that it was a large van and we were the only passengers. The vehicle had two long bench seats so that we both could lie down. We slept the whole way there, rolling in about eleven that morning.

The town was basically a collection of cross streets filled with tourist service buildings and small lodges, all built in the bottom of a bowl-shaped valley. On all sides were huge, towering red mountain peaks, including, toward the southeast, the Sinai range.

We called around on a pay phone until we found a small lodge nearest to Mount Sinai, and by the time we walked into the tiny office to check in, the pace of travel had taken its toll. My energy had fallen substantially, so I went though my mental checklist of Integrations to get centered: expect intuition and Synchronicity, stay in

Alignment, and come back to a love Connection. Now, I added one more: intend Oneness.

When we rang the bell on the attendant's desk, we were greeted by a distinguished-looking older gentleman with gray hair. He spoke perfect English but at first seemed extremely cautious, asking us many questions about our travel plans and passports. Yet by the time we finished checking in, he was smiling and extremely friendly.

He gave us our keys, and then, as we were walking away, he looked thoughtful for a moment.

"If you care for a hike," he said, "there is a trail just outside that leads to a nearby hill. It provides a splendid view of the town and the Mountain of Moses."

We thanked him and headed down the long hall to our rooms, which we found perfectly placed directly across from each other. Even better, my room had an outside door, which opened on to a small patio. We could see the walkway to the hill across the street.

"This is great," Coleman said.

After showers, we walked next door and had a great meal in a little restaurant. When we finished, I asked, "What do you get when you tune in to whether we should contact the flight attendant's brother, Joseph?"

He thought for moment. "I get the feeling we should do it. It's logical and also feels right."

I grabbed my phone and texted Joseph that we had met his sister-in-law and asked if we could talk to him about the Document. I left the phone on so we'd hear the reply if one came in.

"Okay," Coleman said. "Let's hike this hill."

The day was beautiful. The sun shone brightly, with small puffs of white clouds dotting a crisp blue sky. As we walked, we gazed out at the red mountains rising all around us.

"Wow," Coleman said. "This looks a lot like Sedona."

We followed the trail over to the hill and started up, truly amazed by the colors in the rocks themselves. Along with the red were streaks of gray and gold. With every step I began to feel better.

"This hill *feels* like Sedona, too," Coleman said.

At a certain point, the path meandered by a flat ledge that overhung the city, so we stopped and looked down at the town. Just as I was immersing myself in the vista, I noticed Coleman nodding toward something up ahead.

On the other side of the overhang was a rounded protrusion of rock, and on top, a man was kneeling alone on a prayer cloth. He had long dark hair and a short beard and was looking out into the distance toward the southeast. Without seeing us, he turned to a seated position, pulled out a cell phone, and entered in a number.

Suddenly, my text ring went off on my phone. When the man heard it, he whirled around and saw us, a puzzled look on his face. The text read:

My sister already informed me of your arrival. I would love to speak with you. Please call.

I looked back at him. He was smiling broadly. Coleman laughed out loud. It was Joseph.

Immediately, the man jumped up and walked over to us.

"Quite good timing," he said with a thick Egyptian accent. "I'm Joseph. Glad to meet you."

Coleman gave me a look to remind me to practice Oneness, and I immediately held that intention, introducing both of us and telling Joseph that we were looking for some of our friends who had joined a group studying the Document here in St. Katherine.

"I know one group here," he said. "But tell me, how far along are you with the Integrations?"

"We've formed a template group," I said, "and are tuning in to our Guidance. We've just begun Oneness."

"So you've just begun the Eighth step," he said, as though more was coming.

"That's right," Coleman replied.

Joseph asked me to describe Tommy and Rachel to him and when I did, he looked surprised.

"I think I know who your friends are," he said. "I haven't met them yet, but they are here. I will take you to them."

He took one last look out toward the mountains.

"Which peak is Sinai?" I asked.

He pointed farther toward the southeast. "Jebel Musa? That's it right there. Just to the right of St. Katherine's Cathedral."

We stared at it for a long time, and as I tuned in, I thought I felt a calming, welcoming sensation. A flash of memory suddenly broke through, and I realized I was getting a hint, once again, of that mysterious point of Connection I had experienced on Secret Mountain.

"I noticed," I said to Joseph, "that you were kneeling toward Mount Sinai when we walked up."

He smiled. "Oh, no. I was looking toward Mecca. From here, Mecca is almost exactly on the other side of Jebel Musa. But when I'm in prayer, the two places feel aligned inside me."

He looked closely at Mount Sinai again. "It is said that Moses looked upon the face of God there. Wouldn't you love to experience that?"

In just thirty minutes, we were pulling through the gate of a large gray stone house about a mile away from the hotel. Joseph had driven us in his Toyota SUV.

At that moment, I was hit by a stark realization. I was about to see Rachel again. Would I be able to open up to her in Oneness? Or would I feel the same old hesitation? I knew we had connected spontaneously on Secret Mountain, but since then, for some reason I had still resisted opening up to her. The Connection seemed too deep, or would lead to complications or something.

As we got out of the vehicle, the door of the house flung open and Rachel and Tommy rushed out to greet us. I rubbed Tommy's head and embraced Rachel, but I cut it short and again avoided prolonged eye contact with her.

Coleman came along and swept Rachel into a big hug. He among everyone seemed to be the most excited about the reunion, and as we walked toward the house, he confided in me about his feelings.

"I grew up with cold scientists as parents, bless their hearts," he said. "I've never had a real family before."

Inside, we walked into a great room that was filled with nice leather furniture and Persian rugs. A dozen more people were waiting for us, all of them looking toward me intensely, and I looked away from them as well.

Tommy was suddenly tugging me by the arm, taking me over to meet his mother. When we were close enough, I introduced myself and Tommy said her name was Love of Mountain.

"Tommy has told me about all of you," she said, her arm around her son. "Now I know why he didn't want to come with me originally. He must have known he was going to meet you."

"Why *did* you come to St. Katherine?" I asked her.

She looked at me proudly. "To visit my namesake," she said. "Sister Mountain. My father, who was a trader, brought me here when I was young, and it was love at first sight. Secret Mountain and Jebel Musa have the same energy. They both open you up." Tommy was nodding.

A question came to my mind then with such force that I just blurted it out. "Why doesn't Tommy have a Native American name, like you?"

She smiled at Tommy. "Because he is stubborn."

"They have tried to give me names," Tommy reacted, "but none of the names have been right. When I do something important, I will know my tribal name."

Then, as though suddenly thinking of something to do, Love of Mountain rushed out of the room, leaving Tommy and me alone. He looked at me as though he had something to say. I beat him to it.

"Tommy, I have to know how all this relates to the Mayan Calendar. You know, don't you?"

"Yes," he said. "We need to hurry."

He led me through an open entrance into a large sunroom of solid glass walls, and we sat down at a table. I could see Coleman in the other room talking with Rachel and several of the new people. For an instant my eyes met Rachel's again. The room was busy behind them, as everyone seemed to be packing for a trip.

"It is the mythology of my tribe," Tommy began, "that the mountains of the Red Rock area of Arizona and the Red Mountains here are all connected.

"Native peoples have always seen mountains as sacred places that lift us above the common awareness to glimpse the sacred spirit. This spirit is now seeking to come closer. The Maya knew this and came to this world to bring the message of the Calendar to us."

"But what is the message, Tommy?" I asked. "The media has twisted it into predicting doomsday. It's difficult to decide whose interpretation to believe."

At this moment, Coleman strode into the room, obviously sensing that we were talking about something important. I saw a flash of impatience on Tommy's small face, which brought up a smile I tried to hide.

"I'm certain I need to hear this," Coleman said urgently.

Tommy and I both gestured for him to sit down.

"The truth of the Calendar is simple," Tommy continued. "It has nothing to do with doomsday. It spells out a timeline for the entire

Cosmos, and the true purpose of human history. The Maya conceive the Universe as being created approximately sixteen billion years ago, but according to them, the creation didn't happen all at once. Their Calendar gives the dates of nine Steps of Creation that will have occurred from the beginning until the Calendar ends by 2012."

He paused and looked at me as if the beginning date of the Calendar was important. I knew why. Only recently have scientists agreed on a date for the beginning of the Universe at the time of the Big Bang, and that date is very close to the one the Maya chose— begging the question: how could the Maya have known the date of the beginning this accurately, centuries ago? Is the rest of the Calendar just as accurate?

"One scholar in particular," Tommy continued, "has spelled out the dates the Calendar has assigned to each step of creation with great clarity. As I said, the first Step of Creation began about sixteen billion years ago, and included the formation of the Universe and the coalescence of matter into galaxies, stars, and planets, and the beginning of life and its development into the first cells and then into more complex organisms. The Second through the Fourth Steps of Creation brought us mammals, anthropoids, and finally, two million years ago, humans.

"At this point, the remaining Steps of Creation focused on the expanding reach of human consciousness, beginning with a tribal awareness and reaching, about 103 thousand years ago, a regional awareness, where humans developed language and began to become conscious of other human groups in a larger geographical area.

"Next in the Calendar came a national awareness, beginning around 3115 B.C.E., where humans organized first into empires and finally into nations.

"Then on July 24, 1755, another step in creation began, yielding a planetary awareness. This was when we first realized we shared a finite planet and began to interact economically across the globe."

Tommy paused to emphasize something.

"It's important," he continued, "to remember that these steps are not just symbolic. They entail an actual shift in our consciousness. When we reached the planetary step, for instance, we gained the ability to tune in to a consciousness that transcended a flat Earth perception. We literally could more readily feel that we were all together on a round Earth, floating through space.

"And the next surge in creation, occurring on January 5, 1999— the galactic awareness—gave us the ability to stretch our consciousness even farther. It lifted us beyond the planet and gave us even more ability to sense the larger Cosmos. This accelerated the shift from a material and secular outlook to a more awakened spiritual state. We more readily knew we were floating around in space with no real understanding of why. We wanted the real truth of our existence. Religion itself came under question because we wanted more complete answers to our inquiries.

"It was this questioning that led to ideological fanatics thinking they had to defend their doctrines and even force them on people, sometimes violently. This galactic perspective began only two years before 2001, when the wars began over whose religion was best."

I just looked at him, having had no idea the Mayan Calendar was so specific in its dating.

"Scholars are still arguing over the dates somewhat," Tommy continued, "but the general outline of creation is most important. They predicted this sequence of human progress centuries ago."

I recalled then that Tommy had mentioned that the Calendar had predicted nine Steps of Creation. He had mentioned only eight. I asked him about it.

"The Calendar predicts another Step of Creation," the young man continued, "one that is already coming and can be felt. It is intended to bring in an ideal world."

I perked up, remembering that Tommy had told the group that

the Calendar was itself a prophecy similar to the end-times visions of many religions. Most of these scriptural Prophecies talked about a coming Messiah figure who would usher in an ideal world, and now he was talking about the Calendar also pointing to an ideal world.

"Tell me more about what the Calendar predicts," I said.

He waved me off with a flip of his hand, obviously wanting to make another point.

"My tribe believes," he pressed, "that this last step will not be imposed on us. Enough of us must learn how to tune in to the next level of creation. And to do that, we must first receive the consciousness the Integrations speak of, beginning with the Integration we're working on now, the Eighth." He was looking at me as though I particularly had to "get it."

We were interrupted then by the sounds of more movement in the other room. Through the door I could see Love of Mountain and several others rolling back one of the Persian rugs and opening a huge trapdoor in the floor. She looked at Tommy, motioning for him to come help her.

Coleman and I both stood up.

"You know what they're doing, don't you?" Coleman said. "They're getting ready to go to the mountain."

"Why?" I asked.

"I don't know, and they don't seem to, either. But they're sure they have to go."

We were walking back toward them when Rachel abruptly appeared and grabbed my arm.

"I have to talk to you," she said forcefully, leading me into the sunroom and out a back door into a garden courtyard. The area was paved with flagstone and surrounded by thick hedges and flowering plants. The aroma of water lilies came from a small pond in the corner.

"Everyone's packing," I said. "What are they planning to do?"

"They're going to Sister Mountain," she replied. "Something's about to happen up there."

"How do you know?"

She looked at me seriously.

"I know quite a lot," she said. "If you weren't avoiding me, you might realize that!"

I just looked at her.

"Why are you avoiding me?" she pressed.

"Because I'm trying to stay in Alignment," I snapped, wanting to run back in the house.

She smiled and looked at me as if I was a child. "If you had just connected enough to really talk to me, you wouldn't be confused about this. Do you know why I'm here, why I'm trying to reach the real you? This isn't about anything romantic. It's about the Integrations.

"The Template of Agreement is not just for resolving the extreme polarization that's occurring in politics and religious ideology. It's also about bridging the myth and polarization that keep men and women apart."

She shook her head. "You know what I was taught as a child by my mother? That men and women are completely different animals, with a different outlook and language, and doomed forever to misunderstand and manipulate each other. She taught me to lie and control to get what I wanted from men, and as I tried to manipulate my way through one failed relationship after another, I grew to hate men for making me do that.

"And I hated my mother for not preventing the world from being that way. I quit speaking to her for years... and then she died before I could get back home to talk to her."

She looked over at me and I tried to stay with her gaze.

"I know now," she said, "that it wasn't her fault. I wasn't the only one with this misunderstanding. We all play the game of sex and security. You think you have to be in control so you limit your connection with me, or manipulate it in some way. But the fact is, this habit of closing off to some women is something you've probably always done.

"I bet you've never really opened up to any woman. You were busy manipulating, hoping to entice them into a relationship with you, or, on the other hand, dismissing them altogether if they didn't seem like a sexual possibility. We're all stuck in not fully connecting with those of the opposite sex—women using their sexuality to manipulate men, men manipulating women to get sex. But now, as we figure out how to really tune in to each other, we're on the verge of being able to blow past sexual manipulation altogether."

I was watching her speak, struck by her open, authentic expression of all this. It was done with a deep soul Connection to me—yet it was a Connection that meant nothing more than that: deep Connection.

"How did you get so clear about this?" I asked spontaneously.

"My mother told me."

"I thought you said she died before you could speak to her."

"She did."

I just looked at her, thinking of the implications of her remark. And in that moment, I realized that my fear of connecting with her seemed to be fading.

"I'll tell you soon about my communication with my mother," Rachel went on. "But that's not what we need to be doing now. This distance between men and women has to be healed. For most of us, it's been romance or nothing when it comes to the opposite sex. And we can't go forward into another elevation of consciousness until this changes.

"If a template group works at all, it's because it sets a new pattern by agreement and sends that energy out into the world, to help set a new cultural standard in the collective mind. So what you and I heal here and now influences the world in that way. We have to get back to where we were on Secret Mountain. We have to be souls to each other!"

She reached into a large satchel that she carried and pulled out about a dozen crumpled pages. "I don't know how much of the Eighth Integration you've read. But here it is."

I found a bench near the fountain and began to read where I had left off. It immediately held me spellbound.

To completely join minds, it said, we must intend Oneness, but we must also come back to a love state that totally transcends sexual complexity. It named this emotion Agape.

I looked away for a moment and thought about the word. *Agape* was Greek, and it meant a particular kind of love: one of the soul for all of creation, but most particularly, a love for other people that is platonic in nature. Centering in this kind of love, the Document went on, even more than intending Oneness or Conscious Conversation, lifted those in interaction into their highest soul wisdom. Moreover, this elevation was multiplied many times when practiced by a group.

I put down the pages then and walked into the other room, finding Rachel standing in the doorway waiting for me. Our eyes met, and this time I just let myself go fully into her eyes, setting the intention for Oneness and opening to love.

Suddenly, I felt a perceptible movement in my heart, a surge of emotion that created an even greater centeredness and freedom from apprehension that I hadn't experienced since Secret Mountain.

It was right, and totally in Alignment in every way, and never had to be defended. It was Agape.

In my peripheral vision, I noticed a few people in the other room looking at us, but I remained focused on Rachel. She rushed up to me and turned me in the other direction to face the windows that overlooked the courtyard.

"Look how beautiful it is outside," she said. "Remember how the world looked on Secret Mountain? We're truly working our way back there with each Integration. The next step is opening our senses fully to the way the world really looks when we're all connected together in a state of love."

For a moment I took in the beauty. But part of me didn't want to go there yet. All I wanted was to experience this level of Agape again.

I turned around to face Rachel.

I wanted to ask her another question, but the power of the eyes staring at us from the other room was drawing me to them. Everyone was crowded into the doorway looking at the two of us, including Coleman, who was jumping up and down near the back, waving the pages of the Document he held in one hand.

I returned their gazes with the same deep Agape I had projected toward Rachel, and without paying the slightest attention to who was male or female. The energy level and Agape with the group exploded within me even more. They all seemed delighted.

"Wow," I said out loud.

Rachel came around, stood beside me, and looked at the others.

"Every time," she said, "that someone integrates Agape for the first time, it creates a ripple of heightened love in everyone around them, like heat in a greenhouse—or a conversion experience in a crowded country church."

OPENING TO PERCEPTION

For twenty minutes, I walked around and talked with everyone I had met in the group. All of them took time for me, even as they hurried to pack. Most spoke English, but they also easily and spontaneously interpreted for each other as a matter of course.

Together, they reflected a rich cross section of life in the region, from bakers to teachers to engineers, and represented most of the known traditions and sects. To a person, they had experienced a Breakthrough Connection in their own way and were proceeding through the Integrations one by one. As we talked, I realized we were becoming a larger template group.

In fact, many voiced that Agape between people was primarily a concept that had grown out of Western, Judeo-Christian thought. But those in other traditions pointed out that their histories were also full of icons that emphasized the importance of soul love. I myself was aware of a concept in Eastern thought, from Jainism, called Ahimsa, which, if not considered academically identical, was the same in practice. We finally agreed that while most traditions pointed to this level of Connection in some way, the Christian and Eastern religions seem to give it the most emphasis.

At one point, I looked at my phone and found Wil had texted, saying that he had arrived safely and had experienced the Eighth Integration with a smaller group in Cairo. Hira had also communicated, saying much the same thing. She had found another template group of her own in Jerusalem. Both she and Wil had come to the same agreement about the Eighth Integration as those of us here.

Soon after, Adjar texted as if on cue. He, too, agreed with our conclusions, and took the time to express the difficulty his tradition seemed to have with Agape love, especially between men and women who were not married. He mentioned some minority views in this regard that he thought would now be getting more attention.

I sat down by myself to think for a moment, still high from the Oneness and Agape that had elevated us. The honesty and wisdom of Rachel, I knew, had changed me dramatically, and I knew I would never experience conversations with women in the same way again.

Of equal impact was the summary of the Mayan Calendar Tommy had provided. While he didn't finish telling me about the predicted last Step in Creation, I understood even more why he had earlier called the Calendar a prophecy. The remaining last Step in Creation was thought to be a coming wave of Divine creation, one that was meant to somehow move us toward this more ideal world so many were sensing.

I began, then, to notice people walking around the house looking at the paintings and plants in a particular way. Some of them went out to the sunroom and stared at the hazy sunset through the glass. After a while, I realized they were trying to see more beauty. This made perfect sense. The group here seemed to have completed the Eighth Integration and was moving on to the Ninth.

The observation brought back the memories of the search for the Ninth Insight of the old Prophecy. Back then, the old Prophecy found in Peru had predicted that one day we would begin to see the world as immensely beautiful and even light-filled.

I was now sitting on the arm of a chair in the great room, and Coleman came in and sat on the sofa across from me, as if he had something to say.

"Some of the people in this group," he said, "have already begun to integrate the Ninth. They're pretty far along."

He looked at me as though he expected I would pick up on his next statement.

I nodded. "And the Document is talking about a practical way to sustain the experience."

"That's right! And some of them are scientists! They think that opening to perception is built into the structure of our brains, just like the rest of the jumps in consciousness we've experienced. They now believe every step is archetypal and, in a sense, a higher kind of Alignment that we're called to maintain."

That jolted me. A group of scientists were asserting this, based on the similarity of spiritual experience for all of us! I wondered suddenly just how widespread this perception was becoming.

"That's why," Coleman continued, "groups are the best way to proceed now, because as one person in the group gets it, others see the new consciousness and feel it, and pretty soon everyone has fired up that part of his or her brain. This way, it all gets proven to oneself very quickly. It's the process behind the idea of a positive *contagion* of consciousness.

"The Document," he continued, "says that to see more beauty is to get closer to the consciousness that exists in Heaven. There, people know how to use the power of Agape with everyone, especially those locked in ideologies. The Document says to reach those in fear and anger we have to do what they do in the Afterlife.

"It says the Ninth Integration is an important step toward doing that. It gets us closer to a heavenly level of consciousness. This is the secret of reaching those in fear and anger. We have to be able to lift them toward this state."

"How do we do that?" I asked.

He shrugged.

I noticed then that he had a folder with him. "You have the Document?"

"Part of it," he said. "Want to read it?"

As I read, the Document spoke exactly to Coleman's point. Agape, it stated, was easy to accomplish with people who loved you back. It was more difficult with those who were more ideologically opposed. The only way to reach everyone, as Coleman had mentioned, was from an elevated position of consciousness closer to the Afterlife.

Suddenly, we began hearing more noise and movement behind us. All the others were no longer just talking and working. They were moving heavy packs and foodstuff out the door toward the vehicles.

Coleman and I looked at each other, and I was about to go back to reading when the thought came to me to check the phone for texts. I found a message from Adjar. A former insider with the Apocalyptics had told him the extremists knew we were in St. Katherine. They were planning to stop us from getting to the mountain.

"I guess that's why," Coleman said, "the people here are hurrying so. They must have already sensed danger. I'll go tell them what we found out."

Wanting to think about the situation, I nodded and watched him walk off. Neither Coleman nor I had experienced a premonition of trouble. So I tuned in to whether I could picture us going to the Mount. I easily saw the journey and felt it was the right thing to do, but when I attempted to visualize us making it all the way to the summit of the mountain, I couldn't. I tried again with no success.

Uh-oh, I thought, and dashed outside where everyone was gathering around the vehicles, obviously checking in with each other to see who had the best intuition going forward.

What happened next was one of those fast-paced moments of Synchronicity and intuition where everyone spoke at exactly the right time and with perfect clarity about the hunches they were receiving. And it was virtually unanimous. Everyone saw that we were right to head to the Mount, but once there, we should be very careful.

Suddenly, Rachel walked to the center of the group, eager to say something more.

"We can't let these threats," she said forcefully, "interrupt our progress with the Integrations. If we stay in Agape, we'll find a way to stop this danger. Remember where we are. The Ninth Integration says we have to use Agape to pull the Apocalyptics into a higher state and out of their ideology somehow."

There was silence, then Tommy added, "We will discover how to do that at the Mountain. The next step is to tune in to sacred nature, open our perception, and get closer to the spirit world. This ability has long been the emphasis of Native peoples. If we pay close attention, the Mountain will show us the way."

Most everyone agreed to go, despite the danger. But some didn't, feeling their paths took them elsewhere. They would hold us in prayer, they said, leaving twelve of us to load into three vehicles: Joseph's Toyota, Love of Mountain's Subaru, and an old Volvo belonging to one of the others. Coleman, Rachel, and I rode with Joseph.

The plan was to separate and meet at a specific location that Tommy's mother had suggested: the head of a little-known trail that led up the southeastern side of Mount Sinai. Love of Mountain had told us this route would still be guarded by Egyptian troops, but at least it would be less traveled. Because of the layout of the town, we would have to drive west and then south to hit the trail to Sinai.

The trip to the trailhead should have taken, at most, thirty minutes, but as we traveled, we ran into one traffic jam after another. Now we were waiting, again, in a long line of cars to make a turn.

"This little town has really filled up," Coleman said. "I looked up St. Katherine on the Internet before we got here. They average plenty of visitors to Mount Sinai over the course of a year, but nothing like these numbers. There must be an extra thousand people here."

I looked closely into the vehicles around us and at the pedestrians lining the streets. They all looked primarily Middle Eastern, but a good fourth of them were international, with lots of Europeans and North Americans among them.

"You think they're here because of the Document?" Rachel asked.

We all looked at one another.

"Maybe we should stop and ask some of them," I said.

"I don't think so," Coleman retorted. "We should get into the mountains as soon as we can."

All of us agreed, and we headed south, finally moving out of town and into a flat, rocky desert that was alive with small round plants and scrubby bushes that seemed to be glistening in the fading light.

Just like Sedona, I thought.

In twenty minutes, we were approaching the trailhead, and the reality of our situation was sinking in: we were about to scale a mountain in a foreign country without permission, facing a group of extremists who had already tried to kill us.

I shook my head, holding on to my energy level and reminding myself again that there was no choice. To have any chance of reaching the extremists, we had to get up this Mount and finish the Integrations.

"I have a brother who is a high-ranking officer in this region," Joseph said abruptly. "I wanted all of you to know, because he could possibly help us. He has been very extreme at times, but I've been trying to convince him of the Document's importance."

We all looked at one another, and for some reason I felt his brother would be instrumental in whatever happened on Sinai.

"I also know your friend Hira," he continued, "from when I lived in Jerusalem during my youth. My mother was Jewish, and she knew Hira's mother. We all studied end-times Prophecy in the Bible and the Torah. I think the most fascinating aspect of the prophetic literature, however, is that the prophecies of all three major religions seem to have the same structure. Each has an idea of a final conflict, or Armageddon. And each has the notion that a Divine Messiah figure is coming to establish an ideal, spiritual world."

I remembered what Tommy had told me. The next step of Creation of the Mayan Calendar also seemed to have a similar structure. What was Synchronicity trying to show us here?

"It's fascinating," Joseph went on. "And some of the traditions also agree that the same literal events must take place before Armageddon begins. The first event is that the Jews must return to the Holy Land, which has occurred. Then the rebuilding of David's temple in Jerusalem on the site of its old foundation must take place."

"Trouble is," Rachel interjected, "the Dome of the Rock, an especially important mosque, already occupies that site."

"Any reason that both the mosque and the temple couldn't fit up there?" I asked.

They all looked at me in silence.

"The problem," Rachel finally said, "is that the two religions both claim title to the entire rock."

"That's right," Joseph added. "And many believe an attempt to rebuild the temple would signal the onset of Armageddon and the whole end-times drama would be played out, including the coming of the Messiah figures. For our tradition, it would be the Twelfth Imam who would return."

He glanced at Rachel. "You might argue that it would be the return of the Christ."

"Wait a minute," Coleman remarked. "So you're saying that these events—Jews returning to the Holy Land and the rebuilding of David's temple in Jerusalem—are the primary events in prophecy that would signal the beginning of Armageddon?"

"I would add one more from the Arab side," Joseph said. "One of our prophets said the end times are near when there is chaos and incivility building in society, and a general dishonoring of all people. It is a time when the truth is disregarded for more convenient lies."

"You mean runaway ideology?" Coleman remarked.

Joseph nodded. "Yes."

I perked up. The energy of this conversation had begun to feel numinous, and I knew it was happening for a reason.

"There is also another event," Rachel interjected, "that many believe will occur as the end times approach. In Christianity it is called the Rapture, but other traditions have a similar idea as well. It's the notion that as the Messiah figure begins to come to Earth and Armageddon begins, the true believers' bodies will be lifted into spirit and they will meet the coming God figure in Heaven, where they will be protected."

She looked at Joseph.

"Yes, that's right," Joseph said. "In our religion, it is thought that as the Twelfth Imam approaches, our true believers will be taken to the side in spirit and also protected."

Coleman looked around at each of us. "This is amazing. I've never put this together before. All the major religions do have almost the same structure for the end times, just with different names."

*   *   *

Our discussion was interrupted as Adjar turned off the main road onto a bumpy gravel track that left a plume of dust swirling up behind us in the fading light. Within minutes, we were stopping at a place where the road widened into a turnaround and proceeded no farther.

"This is where Love of Mountain said to meet," Joseph said.

We waited another ten minutes before we saw the muted headlights of a vehicle approaching.

"That's Love of Mountain's Subaru," Rachel commented.

Seconds behind them came the Volvo. When everyone was out and ready, Tommy prepared us for the route ahead, telling us the first mile would be relatively flat desert, but the second would be very mountainous and would take us up the southeastern side of Mount Sinai. His mother suggested we hike in for a short distance under the cover of darkness, and then sleep before attempting to move up the mountain.

"What about the Egyptian guards you mentioned?" I asked.

"We will come to a guard station," she replied. "Before we can go past it we must open our perception and learn from those in spirit."

Without saying anything else, Tommy and his mother set a rapid pace through the desert. Eventually, we came to an area where the terrain inclined upward and we began to see enormous boulders dotting the landscape. After another hundred yards, we came to a group of the big rocks circled together. Tommy led us through the maze until we came to an open, sandy area completely surrounded by the rocks.

"We can camp here," he said.

Rachel and I pitched our tents beside each other, and I could see Tommy was intentionally laying out the tent he shared with his mother beside Rachel's as well.

When the tents were up, I built a small fire from the dead limbs of some scrub bushes that grew around the edges of the boulders, realizing as I did so that the circle of huge rocks was reflecting back at us in the light of the moon, creating what felt like a curtain of security.

Rachel seemed to be looking out at them as well and glanced at me as she took out a small cooker and began making freeze-dried stew near the fire. I sat down beside her.

"You know," she said, "Native Americans never camp somewhere unless it has high energy. I talked to Tommy's mother, and of all the mountains she has visited, the Sinai group are her favorites."

Rachel shot me a smile. "She said they are the easiest to light up."

The next day, I was first to awaken. As I climbed out of the tent, only a partial light was appearing in the east. Gathering up some more wood, I stoked the fire and sat down. Traces of red sunlight began to highlight the swirls of clouds overhead.

Tommy's mother came out of her tent, walking around as though she was looking for something. She left the circle of rocks and was gone a long time before returning. Several other people were now out of their tents as well.

She finally walked over to me and asked, "Have you seen Tommy? He left sometime during the night."

"What?" I said, jumping up.

She waved her hand as if to calm me down.

"Don't worry. He's done this before. We've been here many times and he knows the area well, so unless you sense something different, I think it is best to just wait for him to return."

I tried to tune in, but I couldn't really concentrate. I didn't know how she could be so calm. We had just been warned that the Apocalyptics were still looking for us, and anything could happen out there. She left to tell the others as Rachel walked up and sat beside me.

"What's going on?" Rachel asked.

I told her that Tommy had left.

"By himself? Shouldn't we go looking for him?"

"His mother doesn't seem that worried. She wants to wait and see if he will return."

Rachel nodded and sat down, and our gazes met. There was no reluctance on my part, and we held the stare until we both smiled. Suddenly, I saw an image of Tommy in my mind's eye. He was higher up in the mountains...and I was with him!

The vision was clearly an intuition, and I looked back at Rachel, who was now deep in thought herself, appearing slightly sad.

"I think I should go look for Tommy," I said. "What about you?"

She shook her head, still looking away. "I have to stay here."

I gathered my pack, and Rachel walked over to her tent and returned with a feather.

"This is a feather guide that Wolf gave me," she said. "He joked that it was useful to bring two spirits back together, and that I would know what to do with it when the time came."

She handed the feather to me, and I took it and smiled, then turned to go.

"Before you leave, I want to tell you something," she said. "Don't forget where we are in the Integrations. We have to open our perception as quickly as we can." There was still a hint of sadness.

"I saw you tuning in just now," I said. "Did you see something?"

A tear was rolling down her cheek, but she shook it off and put on a happy expression.

"Don't worry, I'll see you when you get back. The feather will see to that."

She gave me a hug and teasingly pushed me on. "You better hurry. We all have a destiny to complete."

As I was walking away, Tommy's mother walked up and seemed to know what I was doing. She described the general route toward the area of the guard station, and wished me well. She added that she was sure everything was all right, and that Tommy would be somewhere in that general location. There seemed to be a good reason in her mind that she was not going herself.

When I passed the last of the giant boulders and was starting up the incline, someone else suddenly called from behind me. I turned to see Coleman running up with his pack on.

"I'm supposed to go with you," he said.

I reached out to grab his arm, once again tremendously glad for his company. He gave me a determined look, and we locked in the Agape.

"Has anyone been talking about the Ninth in camp?" I asked.

"Not much, but they're all studying it. Tommy seems to already understand it the most."

I nodded, and we both walked on without talking, heading east toward the rising spires of rock. After about a half mile, we made our way up a steep ridge that jutted out toward the east, so that we could look out on the ascending waves of ridges and crevices rising up before us. At the top was a crown-shaped summit.

"That's Mount Sinai," I said.

"And there's the guard station right there," Coleman replied, pointing directly below us to a cement-block building located in a small, flat area in the ridges. Several large antennas rose from its tile roof, and we could hear the faint hum of a gasoline generator. Two soldiers talked and smoked cigarettes outside. We both sat down on some rocks and looked the place over. The building was large enough to house perhaps twenty soldiers.

Just then we heard someone call out from above us. The voice was barely audible. We surveyed the area until we saw someone waving about two hundred feet up the slope. It was Tommy.

We hurried up the hill and soon were looking at his smiling face. He offered us some water from a metal cup, and we took it. The water was wonderfully cool.

"Where did this water come from?" I asked.

"Right over there," he said. "You can fill up your canteens."

The crystal-clear water came out of the rocks and then rippled down about twenty feet before disappearing into a crevice.

"I thought there was no water in this desert," Coleman said.

"They call it the spring of Moses," Tommy replied.

Coleman and I just looked at each other.

I caught the youth's eye. "You're up here for some reason, Tommy. What are you doing?"

He looked toward the guardhouse. "Several months ago, I met one of the officers of the guard station. I believe he thinks I'm a wanderer or a prophet or something. I had run out of water and he told me about the spring. I have talked to him several times on my trips here. He knows about the Document but he has always been very secretive. I also believe he knows Joseph's brother."

"What?" I said, glancing over at Coleman. "Joseph said his brother was a high-ranking officer here, a commander."

"I have seen a big man who looked highly ranked talking to my friend."

I looked at Coleman. "Where was Joseph this morning?"

"He had already left camp," Coleman replied. "His tent was next to mine and I woke up as he walked off. It was still dark."

"Have you seen Joseph up here today?" I asked Tommy.

He shook his head. "No one has been here, except for the two soldiers down below."

"We could probably sneak past those two," Coleman said.

"It is not time," Tommy admonished. "We won't be allowed up the mountain until we first learn to *see*."

For a long time, we stayed where we were. Tommy said we must wait until the sun was in the correct position before trying to open up our perception. When the sun was near setting, he explained, it radiated a light of mystery, and extraordinary events could take place.

Coleman and I spent most of the day talking about the old Prophecy and what had occurred in Peru. In the Ninth Insight, the Prophecy had predicted that humanity would slowly increase its energy level and would systematically raise its level of perception. The question was how to practice this ability. We talked about this for a long time, sharing a granola bar for lunch, and waited patiently for the sun to lower in the sky. Finally, the time came, and Tommy told us to gather all our belongings. The sun was barely above the horizen.

"This is the hour that has the most magic," he repeated. "A human can do things at this time of day that can't be done at any other time. Just look out at this light."

Tommy was pointing toward the east where everything was now bathed in a golden-colored aura, and the sky had turned a darker blue. The swirling clouds overhead were now taking on rich browns and streaks of orange. What struck me most was how the light reflected on the rock and sand, bringing out even more rippling highlights.

"Let's walk south down to the desert floor," Tommy said. "We can see better there."

Tommy led us through the rocks along a different route from the one Coleman and I had traveled, winding along the spires and shelves and sheer drop-offs in a much more efficient manner, as though following a hidden trail that Coleman and I could not detect.

When we arrived at a flatter area, he stopped and sat down, looking back at Mount Sinai. Now the sun was hidden completely and the whole scene was cast in an even more mysterious tone. We sat down beside him.

"Look out at Sister Mountain," he instructed, "and focus on it completely. Look at the lines the shadows draw."

This captured my interest, and I began to see the huge range as having a particularly unique form. It came to me that every mountain range of this sort, rocky or wooded, had different lines created by its shadows. Because of this, every mountain system has an entirely unique countenance.

"Now, tune in to its beauty," Tommy said, "and feel Agape in relationship to it."

I was reminded of my experience in Peru at Viciente when attempting to see the auras, or halos, around plants. But I had the feeling Tommy wanted us to see something more fundamental in the landscape.

I focused intensely on the beauty of the mountain and tried to see it as one expressive form. And then a wave of Agape for the mountain gushed forth inside me. Coleman and I looked at each other. He was feeling it, too.

"Now look at the plant right here in front of us," Tommy commanded. "See *its* uniqueness and beauty in Agape."

He was talking about a short, compact, round bush that looked like a miniature tumbleweed. It was no more than three feet in front of us. I tuned in to the plant and looked for its beauty. As before, my emotions exploded with Agape.

"Now look back at the mountain again," Tommy said, "and see

its increased color and form, as if it now has greater majesty in your field of vision."

Just as Tommy said that, the mountain literally jumped out in color and impressiveness. I looked at Coleman, and he shook his head in wonder without turning, showing me he was seeing this as well.

I then noticed that while I was looking at Coleman, I could sense where the mountain was, although I was not looking at it. I was feeling it in the exact same way I could feel my hand behind my back, only with greater intensity.

"Now look back at the plant and feel its impact on your emotions," Tommy instructed. "Everything in our perceptual field has more than an appearance, it has an emotional identity as well—what the Ninth calls a Feeling Identity."

Instantly, I realized the small plant did have an emotional identity, just as with the mountain. I experienced a sudden insight into why we all have favorite furniture, or come back to a familiar vista over and over. Objects have an identity that touches us emotionally.

"Now, switch your focus back and forth between the mountain and the plant."

I did just that, focusing on and feeling the mountain far away, and then the plant close to us. At first nothing of note occurred, then suddenly, I could see them both in a new, amazing way—in what I could only describe as being equally in focus at the same time.

I jumped to my feet and looked all around, realizing that everything was in the same hyperfocus all around me, which created an enhanced, three-dimensional effect. Everything stood out with incredible clarity of color, form, beauty, and existence—all at the same time. And more, it seemed to stretch my consciousness, so that I felt as though I could reach out and touch the farthest cloud or rocky peak.

And then I remembered my experience on Secret Mountain, when I broke through to an apprehension of cosmic space. I was regaining that same consciousness now.

Tommy noticed and said, "It's the consciousness that has begun to become accessible as the next step of creation approaches."

Coleman was now walking around, looking in all directions as well. The thought came to me that we were seeing in expanded 3-D, like in the movies. I wondered if the development and growing popularity of 3-D movies was coming from an unconscious intuition that we were nearing the ability to see that way ourselves. Was another pathway popping open in the human brain?

The remarkable aspect of this way of seeing was that it seemed so easy and natural at this point. Coleman grabbed my arm and looked at me, beaming.

"This is the way it was on Secret Mountain," he said, "only it seems more normal now."

That was the word: *normal*. On Secret Mountain, the effect still carried a slight mind-blowing or adrenaline feeling. But now it was calming, if anything, and felt perfectly real, as if we were already integrating it as a way of perception we could sustain in daily life.

Besides the three-dimensionality, another enhancement was that my eyes now seemed to have an advanced acuity in which everything was more clear and lit up, as though I'd suddenly entered an inner-lit wonderland of some kind. And that included our bodies. They literally had taken on a sheen that was more radiant and beautiful. Yet again, it all still felt normal.

Tommy was looking at me with a huge smile, his face also beaming and glistening slightly. We were all in a state of pure love, Agape—with one another and with the beauty and majesty of everything around us.

Suddenly, I thought to check for a text. When I saw one from Wil, I laughed with delight. He said he could feel us reaching the Ninth Integration and had reached it himself. He added that while many other traditions spoke of this kind of perception, the Native traditions by far emphasized this ability to see nature as it really is. He ended by saying he was in contact with someone who knew where the Twelfth part of the Document had been released, and he would be heading to Sinai as soon as he talked to him.

I put the phone away and turned to Tommy. "So have you been seeing this way the whole time?"

"Mostly," he said. "But Agape with Mother Earth has to be maintained and treasured. And one has to eat clean food to remain at this level of perception."

We looked at one another.

"This is the Ninth Integration, isn't it?" Coleman asked.

"Yes," Tommy replied. "To maintain a heightened perception of the world, one needs only to intend to tune in, in Agape, to a new level of beauty, and to practice seeing everything with a single focus. The mountains will light up."

He looked at Coleman. "As you have said, it can be proven to oneself!"

Just then, out of the corner of my eye, I saw something move in the desert, and I jerked around. Nothing was there. Coleman gave me an expression that told me he had seen it, too.

"What was that?" I asked Tommy.

He walked closer to us. "At this level of perception we are much closer to the other side."

"You mean the Afterlife?" Coleman asked. "Heaven?"

"Yes."

Colman glanced at Tommy again. "You think what we glimpsed was a spirit?"

"Yes," Tommy replied, giggling. "But spirits are people, too. And they have something to tell us."

WHAT HEAVEN KNOWS

As much as I wanted to stay in the mountains, it was almost completely dark now, and Tommy said we should go back. I saw a look on his face that concerned me, so I tuned in to our return trek to the Circle of Rocks. I found it difficult to visualize.

After about three hundred yards, Tommy suddenly called for us to stop. He was peering into the distance, listening.

"What's wrong?" I asked.

"I don't know," he replied. "We have to be careful. Keep your energy up."

He looked into the night for a few more seconds then said, "Do you hear that?"

I shook my head.

Tommy began walking ahead. "There are people talking up there somewhere. Let's find them."

We made our way forward for about a hundred feet, coming to a large outcropping about thirty feet high. As we grew closer, I began to hear the talking myself. We climbed up the rock and found a place where we could look over. About thirty feet in front us of was a group of Apocalyptics huddled together, discussing something in loud tones. At the center of the group was their leader, Anish. He was talking to a short, round man in an Egyptian military uniform, telling him something in Arabic.

"I can understand this," Tommy whispered. "That large man is Joseph's brother. He's telling him about the Circle of Rocks and where it is." Tommy looked at us in alarm. "Now they know where our camp is."

A rush of anger moved through me as I remembered Joseph telling us he wanted to contact his brother. Did he give away our location?

"We have to get back!" I said quietly, trying to control myself. "Now! Let's go!"

We made our way back to the circle as quickly as possible, and I was fighting against going into fear. For some reason I began to remember things my father had told me about his experiences in World War II. Getting rid of the fear is impossible, he said. All you can do is focus on what you're doing, and even if people are being killed all around you, you concentrate on the job and get it done. I never quite grasped how he did that.

As we approached the first large boulders of the circle, Coleman pulled me aside.

"You look like your energy is collapsing," Coleman said, obviously trying to look deeply at me to reestablish the Agape connection.

I blew him off. "If the Apocalyptics get there before we do, everyone could be killed."

When we made our way back to the circle we found the others already breaking camp. As I rushed up to Rachel, she noticed the change in me immediately.

"What's wrong?" she asked. "What happened?"

I told her what the Apocalyptics had said, then added angrily, "Joseph's brother has sold us out. Joseph himself could be involved."

"Calm down," she said. "We were all getting the image that we should leave immediately, and we're hurrying as fast as we can. But there has to be some mistake. Joseph would not have told his brother where we were camped."

She pointed to a stack of papers that were lying on a rock near her tent. "Joseph brought us copies of the Tenth Integration he'd found, then left again. He's still looking for his brother. Why would he betray us?"

"I don't know."

Her eyes were drawing me in again, and I felt the Agape and the peace come back a little, but my perception had totally crashed.

"We've been working on the Ninth," she said, "at the same time you three were. We could feel you. You have to hang on to to it. We've even gotten into the Tenth."

"We have to leave now!" I pressed.

"Okay, okay. Here's the rest of your stuff."

She was pointing toward my folded tent and a few other things I'd left behind. While I was packing, she seemed to think of something and ran over, picked up the copies of the Document, and stuffed them into my pack as well.

"There," she said. "You can take care of these for everyone in case something happens."

Her tone was again slightly sorrowful. This was the second time she'd said something like that. I wanted to ask her what she knew, but she had already picked up her own pack and was walking away.

"Come on," she said. "We found a back way out of this circle."

Before I could catch her, she glanced around and her eyes froze on something behind us.

"Do you still have that feather?" she asked.

"Yeah, why?"

She was still staring at something behind me. Whirling around,

I caught sight of the silhouette of a lone figure standing on the huge boulder farthest from us. There was no mistaking that shape. It was Anish.

For a long moment we were frozen, and then Rachel looked at me and said, "Listen. None of us will make it unless I try to reach him. Go on, get everyone out of here."

Without moving, she focused on the leader, and he turned and looked right at her, their gaze palpable in the night. Several others from our group noticed and stopped to look, but Coleman knew what was happening and pushed them on. I yelled at several people closer to me, telling them to get out.

"I'm not strong enough yet," I heard her say, and I turned in her direction. It was already too late. Anish waved his hand, and instantly a flurry of bullets rained down toward us from everywhere, hitting the dirt and the rocks. One hit my pack so hard it knocked me backward into one of the big boulders. The fall dislodged the feather Rachel had given me from my pocket, and it landed on my face.

I grabbed it instinctively, even as I struggled to see in the dust and confusion. Suddenly, I felt Rachel's arms around me, pulling me to my feet.

"This way," she urged.

I realized at some point she had let go of me, and as I stumbled along, my head finally cleared. Surprisingly, I now had perfect clarity and was feeling no fear or anger at all. In fact, my emotional state had inexplicably returned to Agape. The night sky was radiant with moonlight and the rocks were more luminous than ever. I had regained my perception.

Rachel was ahead of me, walking briskly now, and I was able to keep up with no difficulty. I noticed that her body was moving along with unusual fluidity and grace, her clothes looking shiny and reflective. She led me straight to the spot where Coleman, Tommy, and I talked earlier, looking down on the guardhouse. Then she took another, hidden route past the soldiers and farther up toward the summit.

As we walked, I wondered how she knew about this hidden trail. Had Tommy or his mother told her about it earlier?

"Where are we going?" I asked.

"Just up ahead a bit farther," she said.

The sound of her voice was different somehow and shocked me. I was experiencing it as much inside my head as outside. I slowed up and stopped, suddenly disconcerted. She noticed and came back toward me.

"We can go slower if you like," she said. "It just takes a little getting used to."

Her face was now more luminous than ever.

I sat down with a thud and realized my pack was still on my back.

She sat down with one easy move without using her hands, something I'd never seen her do before. And unlike when we were at the circle, her face was totally upbeat now, without a hint of sadness.

"You know where we are, right?" she asked.

"What?"

"We aren't in Kansas anymore."

"What are you talking about?"

She leaned in closer. "Remember I told you that I read the Tenth Integration?"

"Yeah."

"It says if we follow the Synchronicity, we will be able to learn from those in Heaven in a direct way, and that will elevate us into the next level of consciousness."

I nodded for her to go on.

"I never finished telling you about my mother," she began. "I hated her for making a controller out of me and was racked with guilt when she died before I could talk to her. Then, maybe because I was thinking about what I should have said to her, I began to notice little things happening. I would be shopping for shoes and see a pair that looked exactly like the ones she wore. Or I would pass a soap store and smell the fragrance of the very soap she used. At the oddest times, I would hear her favorite old songs.

"And then one day, without anything pointing out the way, I just decided to tell her how I felt out loud, as though she were there. Immediately, I began to intuit what she might say back to me, only I realized it wasn't something I would necessarily have been able to guess. That's when I realized that I was having a real interaction with her.

"The idea of communication with the Afterlife seemed too strange at first, and I stopped for a while, but the memory of the experience was so energizing and profound, I gradually began to communicate with her more often. Eventually, she told me how much she regretted the way she had raised me to think of men. She said it was all a mistake that tormented her, and that she now holds the Agape and speaks from truth—and wishes she had known earlier, so she could have taught me this new way."

I was just looking at Rachel, puzzled.

"Don't you see?" Rachel said. "The Document says we can begin to communicate with those in the Afterlife and clear all our resentments and issues with them. All we have to do is use more of our power to tune in and have a conversation. It's never too late. And there is so much *more* they want to communicate to us.

"In fact, my mother said they desperately need to speak with us, right now, at this crucial point in history. They know the real Plan for the human world, and it's time for us on this side to understand."

She lifted her eyes and looked behind me. I turned around but didn't notice anything. Rachel moved closer, which I experienced as an embrace of some kind, a hug, even though we were still several yards apart.

"Remember what the Ninth Integration talked about?" she asked. "I'm sure Tommy told you. Each item in our surroundings has its own Feeling Identity, its own sense of thereness to us. Well, that's true of humans as well. Every person has a Feeling Identity we can detect emotionally."

I was nodding now, getting it.

"That's why," she continued, "when people close to us die, even when we think we are prepared for it, we are often devastated. What is lost is that feeling that *is* them, something we've always felt and taken for granted. That's why when a loved one dies, people often say it feels as if a part of us dies, too. They're grieving for the loss of that emotional constant that is no longer there."

She paused and again seemed to look past me, and I knew in that instant that we really had crossed the vale somehow. We were in the Afterlife.

"Someone here wants to talk to you," she said, smiling. "Can you tune in to the feeling you remember?"

I knew who it was before she asked. I could smell the cigarettes in his front shirt pocket as though I was back in his lap as a child. I could detect the strength of his being, the way he talked, the child-like laughter of his practical jokes. They were all part of the unique feeling that was him.

Yet at the same time, I realized that part of him had changed— gone was the nervous anger and frustration that he displayed every morning of my youth, forcing everyone to walk on tiptoes in his presence or face the inevitable explosion. And gone as well was the harsh look of disapproval that had instilled in me such a dread and wariness toward others. All of this had been removed.

"It's your father," Rachel said.

When I turned around, there he was, radiant and youthful looking. I was now receiving thought impressions that I knew must be coming from him. He told me that the cause of his behavior—his own early family resentments and wariness—had been resolved in the Afterlife with his own parents. The only part that was still incomplete was his need to resolve the resentments I was holding on to.

"Closing off to others," he communicated, "is a tendency that those in our family inherited, as surely as the color of our eyes. But seeing the history of a problem, and truthfully acknowledging it, allows us to let it go. And now," he went on, "the Afterlife is changing. We don't have to wait until reunion over here. You are close enough to us now to reach out to us, so we can resolve everything immediately. Once those blocks are clear, you can understand what we know."

In an instant, I knew my resentments were gone. I might still go into aloofness out of habit, but less and less without being immediately conscious of it. I knew from the old Prophecy that once we become conscious of the drama we play, its strength diminishes.

With those thoughts, he began to fade until I could no longer see him.

"Wait," I said out loud. "There's more I want to ask."

At that point, I could no longer feel him, and I almost went into the same panic I had felt when he died. I looked at Rachel, whose gaze said to tune in. So I brought back the memory of how it felt when he was present, and immediately he was there, although this time only as a mild distortion in space, like heat waves rising from a hot highway. But it didn't matter. His Feeling Identity was there, and that was the most important thing.

"You mentioned I could understand more," I said to him. "What were you talking about?"

I heard: "Just watch."

*   *   *

After he had gone, I suddenly realized it was dawn and the light was creating even more beauty in the sky and rocks around me.

Turning to look at Rachel, I was jolted. She was now surrounded by several other people. It came to me that the woman closest to her was her mother, and instantly I knew that she and Rachel had had a catharsis similar to the one between my father and me.

I also knew something else: I was being shown all this for a reason. As with my father, her mother had been unable to turn her attention to other matters, because she was so focused on resolving with Rachel. Later, when she and Rachel had cleared the past, they had communicated while Rachel was in the earthly plane and her mother was in the Afterlife. This communication, and others like it, were breaking new ground. The hurt and resentment was being healed across the two dimensions. The significance was that both dimensions of existence had, in that act of reconciliation, been made more free and clear, and thus resonated at a higher level of consciousness with each other.

I tuned in to my father and felt a sweeping confirmation. Many in the Afterlife yearned for the same release of pent-up regrets—for truths not said, for actions not taken, as did those on Earth. And now, with the Integrations lifting our consciousness, we were close enough so that we could communicate across the dimensions. And as a result, both Heaven and Earth were being energized and raised to another level.

Suddenly, I thought of a Bible Prophecy from the book of Revelation about the end times: "...And there will be a New Earth and a *New Heaven*..." Now we knew how this Prophecy was coming true.

With that thought, the action suddenly stopped all around me, and everyone, especially Rachel, turned and looked at me. They all seemed elated at my conclusion.

"You're getting the Tenth Integration," Rachel said. "All you have to do is keep tuning in, and you'll soon know all that Heaven knows."

With that, the group surrounding Rachel started walking down the slope, if you could call it walking. It actually seemed more like gliding. Those who were presumably permanent occupants of the After-life had bodies similar to ours, although they moved along the ground with legs that seemed to merely flicker in the walking motion rather than actually push themselves along the ground. All Rachel and I could do was run as best we could to keep up, although I noticed, after a while, that Rachel had begun to appear the same way as the others.

At this point, it didn't matter. I still had no fear, and as I basked in a full Agape state, I knew without a doubt that I was going to be shown many things here. We walked up the incline through a series of jagged spires and worked our way onto another ledge of rock that had turned-up edges, like the railings of a deck. From here, we could see a magnificent view of Mount Sinai's summit, as well as down toward the trails leading up the mountain.

Suddenly, everyone began watching a troop of Egyptian soldiers huddled together toward the north. Something seemed to have happened to one of the soldiers. They were desperately trying to revive him, wetting him down with water, and fanning him in an effort to cool him off.

"Sunstroke," Rachel said.

Finally, they gave up and covered the body, then lifted him and began carrying him back toward the guard station. We could see dozens of other luminous people walking beside the soldiers, seemingly talking to them. The soldiers, however, could not see them and weren't paying any attention.

"What are they saying to the soldiers?" I asked Rachel.

"Listen for yourself," she replied.

I tuned in to their conversation and instantly knew what was being communicated. The luminous people were using the Oneness Principle and Agape to merge with the soldiers, seeking to increase the consciousness of the military men, hoping they would become aware that they were walking toward danger.

Now I could see why. Forty yards ahead of them were people with weapons, hiding near a rocky mound. I caught sight of several I recognized. It was the Apocalyptics, dozens of them, readying their guns to protect something on the other side of the mound.

"They're running right into the extremists," I blurted, looking at Rachel and the others. They didn't return my gaze. All eyes were resolutely focused on the group of soldiers.

I then looked at the Apocalyptics, and to my amazement saw that they, too, had dozens of luminous individuals encircling them, also attempting to lift them into a larger awareness, wanting them to find their own higher-self Connection.

I realized then that the luminous people wanted the soldiers to see something—a fork in the path ahead that would take them in a more northerly route, out of danger.

I hurried to add my own energy to the effort, going through the procedure of intending Oneness with the soldiers until I could feel the Agape with them. I tried to visualize that they would open up, feel the danger. But the soldiers seemed undeterred, increasing their pace toward the Apocalyptics.

Suddenly, I again felt that comforting sensation that I had experienced when falling as a youth, the one that told me all was going to be okay. I also saw something unusual: flickers of light surrounding the soldiers. For a moment, nothing changed. The captain of the group looked to be leading them straight to their doom. Then, his pace gradually slowed to a halt, and he waved to his men to take the northerly route to safety. A wave of celebration swept through the luminous helpers.

"How did that work?" I asked Rachel.

She said, "The soldiers were being lifted toward a Heaven consciousness, at least a little bit, so that a premonition could come through to warn them."

"Is it a matter of people here just wishing with all their might that a particular outcome will happen?"

"No. In some situations, the best outcome to visualize is obvious. But other situations aren't so clear. Therefore, the people here are purely seeking to join minds with those on the earthly side. Apparently, that's all it takes. A higher consciousness always has the effect of lifting someone at a lower consciousness up to a higher level."

She grinned at me. "As Coleman might put it, if someone who has more pathways activated in the brain merges minds with someone with fewer, the pathways in the person at the lower level tend to pop open as a result of the contagion effect. Of course, there are other ways to amplify our influence even more, as you'll see in the next Integration. But this is the basic way it works."

I already knew the answer but I asked the next question anyway. "What were those flickers of light around the soldiers?"

She gave me a smile. "Angels. They spontaneously come in to help, especially if we remember to request it."

Acting as though she was in a hurry, Rachel suddenly told me there was something else I needed to see. We moved down the slope a bit farther to another area where we could see toward the east, away from Sinai. We sat down without talking and gazed out over the vista of ridges cascading down toward the desert floor.

A movement to my left attracted my attention. We could see a lone soldier stumbling down the rocks as if dazed. He looked much more luminous than the soldiers we'd seen before.

"He must be the soldier who died," Rachel said.

The man suddenly sat down and stared into space without moving.

"What's he doing?" I asked, then remembered to tune in. Immediately, I began to get impressions of what was happening. The man was having a life review, realizing how many opportunities to follow his destiny he had missed or had been too afraid to pursue. His focus shifted to his wife, and I felt his face grimace over how immature he knew he had been, preferring to spend time with his friends and not enough with their five-year-old child.

Yet he was sure the child was the best part of his destiny. He had known from the first moment he had seen his wife that they would marry and have a child, and the child would go on to accomplish many things. He also knew he was supposed to have given his daughter many lessons during her life. How, he wondered, could he do that now. I looked at Rachel.

"He will soon find out how he can help her," she said with twinkling eyes. "Won't he?"

Suddenly, the man jumped to his feet and began looking around wildly.

"What's he doing now?" I asked.

"He knows," she replied, "that there is something unresolved with his father. And he can't find him."

The soldier began to fade until we could barely see him.

"What's happening?" I asked. "Where is he going?"

She looked at me with concern. "You may not want to go there."

"Why?"

"It's not pretty."

Old memories of my experiences with the Afterlife when studying the Prophecy and the Tenth Insight came back to me.

"You're talking about Hell, aren't you?"

She shook her head. "Not in the way most people understand it. It's more like lostness, or being so psychologically repressed you put yourself in a self-imposed limbo."

I decided I wanted to attempt to tune in, and what followed was a journey into coldness and low energy where the man found his father. The father had been a career military officer all his life, with no model for spirituality at all. He had had his chances, as many devout and conscious friends had synchronistically come into his life. Yet he had pushed their messages out of his mind.

After death, his anxiety was so great, he had built an imaginary world around himself of the same unquestioning materialism, with dreamed-up enemies and wars and conquests, all reflecting the exact way he'd experienced such things on Earth. I became aware of the driving force behind this delusion: the Cycle of Revenge. He had kept himself asleep with an overriding hate and desire to pay back those who had killed his friends. And it never ended. He would inflict casualties, and then his enemies would retaliate, then he would seek revenge again, feeling the satisfaction of hurting those who had hurt him.

But as before, I could see many deceased loved ones surrounding the father, seeking to merge minds with him, visualizing that he would be lifted up into his own Connection and awakening. But the father remained steadfast, even though the lack of light was creating an unconscious torment inside him. Finally, the darkness was too much for me, and I looked over at Rachel again, breaking the Connection with the soldier. Taking a breath, I sucked in the warm Agape and appreciated it even more.

"Does anyone ever get out of that place?" I asked Rachel.

"Oh, yes. Everyone has a latent sense that there's something more. The problem is that people who are in fear and ideology bring those same obsessions with them to the Afterlife. That's why it is so important that we stay aligned and help others on Earth to wake up."

She shook her head. "The hardest to reach are those who hold on too tight to various doctrines about spirituality. They think they already know the truth intellectually and forget they have to feel the love and open their consciousness to get to Divine Connection."

"Come on," she said. "There's something more that is known over here."

She led me farther down the slope toward the east, and we came to a flatter area of the mountain, where another group of luminous people stood together focusing on one individual, a woman. She was slightly out of focus.

Rachel smiled as I concentrated on the woman and tuned in automatically, attempting to hear what was going on. Eventually, I began to understand. The person fading was in the process of being born into the earthly dimension.

I looked closer and began to pick up on the intentions of the others standing around the woman. They were supporting her dream for her coming life. Her intent was to help bring a new generation of honest Science into the world. It was clear that this was her way of contributing to the Plan.

The Plan? I turned around and looked hard at Rachel. There it was again, mention of a plan of some kind, apparently known in the Afterlife but not yet fully understood on the earthly plane. Rachel nodded toward the woman.

Concentrating as intensely as I could, I finally began to see her larger contextual understanding of her new life on Earth. It was a much longer sense of history than we had attained at the Second Integration. It encompassed all that had happened in creation, and included the larger meaning behind life itself.

In an instant, I comprehended it. The whole purpose for human existence was to systematically convey the knowledge and consciousness known in the Afterlife into the earthly dimension, so as to bring both dimensions into a full condition of Unity with each other and with Divine Consciousness. She carried this Plan—this larger purpose for life—in her mind as certainly as she knew what she wanted to personally do after birth.

As I tuned in further, I began to see how this drive for Unity had played out in history. It had all started with the creation of the earthly dimension itself, roughly sixteen billion years ago, which established the so-called physical platform for our collective journey. As I watched, the whole story of creation played out in my mind.

In this early Universe, gases and the first chemical elements gravitated together until they became so dense they heated up into stars, which lived and died and spewed new elements into the Universe. On Earth, water and these more complex elements interacted in shallow tide pools, and in the spirit of this urge to Unity, chains of amino acids unified into larger cells. Then these cells began to unify further into multicelled organisms, all in a march toward an ever greater level of complexity and potential for consciousness. Over the millennia came fish then amphibians, reptiles, mammals, and finally humans.

At this point, the focal point of the creation story shifted to humanity. Now the driver of this urge to Unity was an ever-expanding human consciousness of the world around them. Over millennia, individual families came together into tribes and villages, then leaped to regional coalitions, empires, and nations.

And every step of the way, heroes had been born into the earthly realm from the Afterlife—some recognized and some working in anonymity—struggling to push forward these gains in understanding a tiny bit more. Slowly, we moved from the idea of nature deities to Greek-style archetypal gods, and finally into the great truth of monotheism, the concept of one Divine source. Over the years came the three larger religions of Judaism, Islam, and Christianity, each thinking their path was the only way.

With Modern times came the Enlightenment, and Science and a growing urge to unify human understanding. Suddenly, I saw how this planetary consciousness had begun to progress during the later twentieth century into a higher, more galactic perspective, and the questions of life began to arise again in a mass way. What were we doing here? What was the purpose of life?

I could see how this need for clear spiritual answers had created a deep insecurity in the older religions. They felt their doctrines might be questioned or destroyed altogether. Just after the turn of the twenty-first century, the wars had begun over whether one religion could impose itself on the others.

And then I could see that the woman was aware of the Document and the most recent urge to Unity: the Integration of spiritual information into daily life, and into a fully awakened consciousness connected to the one God. She was aware of the efforts to unify religion around the common experience of this Divine Connection and of the emerging Templates of Agreement...and finally, she knew of the Rise to Influence.

For the first time, I saw clearly the long story of creation in its totality. My energy level suddenly elevated, and I knew I was experiencing more of the Tenth Integration. It was the awareness that we had the potential, right now in our lifetimes, to pull this Plan fully into consciousness. It would be the culmination of billions of years of creation.

Yet at the same time, I sensed there was one last aspect of the Plan that I hadn't yet grasped.

"Did you see anything," Rachel asked, "that looked familiar in the Plan you just saw?"

Immediately, I knew her meaning. The steps in the Universe's

long development was very similar to the Steps of Creation prophesied by the Mayan Calendar.

"That's right," she said, reading my mind. "The early Maya had
a breakthrough of their own during their time, when they remembered much of the Plan for creation. Yet their culture was still out of
Alignment, and they knew they couldn't hold on to the knowledge.
So they built the timeline for this Plan into their stone architecture
and inscriptions, hoping that future humans would discover it and
transcribe their message. And that's exactly what occurred."

She paused and looked at me. I could again feel her energetic
embrace.

"But the Maya showed that creation wasn't complete, that
another push was coming in to help us unify completely, if we
came into Alignment and were able to tune in. Some scholars have
called it a Universal Consciousness. Apparently, the Maya thought
of it as the final phase of creation, which will lead the souls in both
dimensions of life toward final completion and Unity. And it will,
if enough of us seek to embrace it."

She looked ready to drive her point home. "We can already fore-
see this force of creation coming, and soon it will be easier to feel.
We all sensed it on Secret Mountain."

Again she paused.

I was electrified now. "You're talking about the point of Connection
I've been trying to figure out all this time. You experienced it too?"

"Yes, the last step in Unity begins with understanding what this
phenomenon is and how to connect with it more fully. We are now
ready to fully discover our spiritual nature, and it will mark the beginning of the last expansion of human consciousness into unification."

Rachel's image was beginning to blur, as though she was fading.

"Remember what we talked about," she continued. "Most of
the Prophecies held by religious traditions have some concept of

the Rapture—acquiring a spiritual body and moving into Heaven, avoiding Armageddon.

"Humans brought these images into earthly culture, because it's also part of the Plan—just not exactly as the prophets have said. It has to be understood symbolically. All those prophecies and scriptural references have come into history from people trying to remember what they knew in the Afterlife, but they didn't get it quite right. The truth came to them through the lenses of their own individual religions, which created all this competition. In reality, the Prophecies are all pointing toward something else, one event meant for everyone."

I still didn't quite get it.

"Don't you see?" she responded. "There's only one Rapture! The Rapture is a bodily transformation that happens through heightened perception and consciousness such as we have glimpsed. We shouldn't be waiting on God to bring the Rapture. God is waiting on us! We have to open up to Divine Consciousness enough so that our perception and energy expand enough so that it can occur. And it may take a long time to achieve. The important part is that we know what we are working on, what our drive to Unity can achieve. And that more help is coming, if we learn how to tune in."

I looked at her, getting it fully. "You're again talking about this Universal Consciousness that the Maya saw."

"Yes, but don't get hung up on a name. It's more personal... and it's the last step in understanding what Heaven knows. We're already sensing..."

Now she was fading almost completely, and I couldn't hear her last comments. All that was coming through was one vague, urgent plea.

"Just do what we do, and raise your Influence," she seemed to be communicating. "You'll understand fully when you grasp the Eleventh Integration and find the Twelfth."

I tried to ask another question, but my eyes would no longer focus. I was spinning away, falling backward into a blinding flash of light.

THE RISE TO INFLUENCE

Hours seemed to pass before I began to hear talking around me. I struggled to open my eyes.

"He's waking up," I heard Coleman yell.

I felt, before I could see, the others gathered around me. I was now at the rock overhang again, overlooking the guardhouse on the southeastern approach to Sinai. I saw my pack lying beside me. The flap had been opened and the copies of the Tenth Integration had been taken out and were lying around. But no sign of Rachel.

I looked down at the feather still in my hand, and in that moment I knew.

"We found you here," Coleman was saying. "You must have hit your head. You've been unconscious."

"Where is Rachel?" I asked.

He reached over and touched my shoulder. The others looked devastated.

"She didn't make it," he whispered. "She was killed at the Circle of Rocks."

I nodded slowly. I knew I should have known the whole time, but I was still thrown into total shock. I was just with her.

I pleaded with him. "Are you sure? She pulled me out of the

Circle during the gunfire. I was with her for a long time. We were able to observe the Afterlife together. We saw the Plan."

"I checked her myself," Coleman said. "And right after, a group of Egyptian soldiers came to investigate the explosions. The Apocalyptics had to back off. So all of us except Rachel were able to get away. You were missing. I saw the soldiers carry her body away. I texted Wil and the others and told them. I'm so sorry."

At this point, I was emotionally swept into one of the most profound feelings of loss I had ever experienced. Rachel's energy had been a part of this entire journey, beginning with our first Connection at the Pub. She was a partner in my clearing to Agape, and now she was gone. My head told me she was still alive in the Afterlife, but I missed her radiant eyes, and the thoughtfulness that had kept me so grounded. Amid tears, I blurted all this out to the others.

Then, right at my darkest moment, I suddenly felt her hug from a distance that I had felt on the other side, and smelled the familiar rose perfume she had always worn.

I knew, then, that she was not only still alive. She was right here with us!

"She helped me through so many things on this trip," Coleman said. "And now she's dead."

"She's not dead!" I protested.

"I know. I know," Coleman said. "I get the Tenth Integration. We were all tuning in to the Plan. But knowing that she still lives isn't the same as having her right here to talk with, or to get one of those famous hugs from."

"No, you don't understand," I shouted confidently. "She's right here with us. Now. She was touching me from a distance in the Afterlife so I would know it was possible here. Tune in! You can still get that hug!"

The others were gathering around closer, listening intently, and they began to sense Rachel as well. For several hours, I carefully

relayed to them everything that had occurred in the Afterlife, especially the Plan and goal of history, bringing to Earth the knowledge
and consciousness known in Heaven, and Rachel's statements about
the coming Universal Consciousness. Tommy smiled at me.

Everyone told me about what had happened here when they had
read the Tenth part of the Document they'd found in my bag. As we
talked, our energy elevated us together into the Tenth Integration.

"It's about realizing that the Afterlife is right here," Coleman
offered. "We can resolve everything with our loved ones and receive
what they know. The key is to do what they do: use their Influence
and the Law of Connection to uplift everyone into a Connected consciousness. It's another level of Alignment."

"Native peoples," Love of Mountain said, "have never lost this
ability to communicate with the other world. Developed cultures
have derided this awareness as ancestor worship, but we have held
this Connection as important since humans became conscious."

She gave us a particular look, and I knew she was right. We were
now in a template discussion. Everyone agreed that the Native traditions had always had the best emphasis on this Integration, although
mystical Christianity and certain Jewish writings in the Kabbalistic
traditions point to Afterlife contact as well.

"Over here!" Tommy's mother was saying. We had all started to
gather our gear, sensing we must move farther up the Mount. We
dashed to the overhang and saw Joseph walking through the gate
at the guardhouse and heading back in our direction. He eventually
stopped and went in another direction for a while, then in another,
apparently attempting to hide his true destination from the soldiers.
When he was out of sight of the guardhouse, we could see him turning toward us again.

"We have to leave before he gets here," Coleman suddenly shouted. "If he was involved in the attack on us, he might have soldiers heading our way right now."

Many of the others seemed just as fearful, and I felt myself moving into deep anger again. My energy plummeted. What if Joseph had been responsible for Rachel's death? What kind of monster was he? Here he was, walking around free and alive, and she was gone. My emotions were moving from anger to a vengeful urge to get back at him.

I suddenly stopped myself, shaking my head. Unconsciously, I had gone into a Cycle of Revenge, just that fast.

Tommy was looking down at Joseph and spoke up. "Wait a minute. He seems to be alone. And I can see no soldiers. I think we should talk to him."

"He's right," I said. "We have to find out the truth."

We all agreed and waited there until Joseph walked up. He appeared shocked that we were now in this location.

"You're here," he said, walking quickly up to us. "I wasn't able to find my brother. No one had seen him. I am afraid he is with the Apocalyptics now." Joseph's face was sad, as though he thought he'd failed.

None of us responded, so he continued, "One of the soldiers at the gate told me my brother had ordered them not to patrol in certain areas of the mountain any longer."

He looked at Tommy. "I think this soldier knows you."

We were still not saying anything.

"Look." Joseph was pointing to his knapsack. "He also gave me this." He was pulling out a stack of papers. "It's the Eleventh Integration! It tells us how to..."

His words trailed off. He could see we were still looking at him intensely.

"What's wrong?" he asked.

Everyone surrounded him and we asked Joseph if he knew

what had happened at the Circle of Rocks. He said he didn't, and when we informed him of the shooting, he was so genuinely shaken he had to sit down—prompting most of the group to welcome him back with hugs and encouragement.

"Joseph," Coleman asked, "why did you come up to this location now?"

"Because the guards said there are many more people coming into town from everywhere. I headed up here because I wanted to see if I could detect anyone coming up from this side."

Coleman and I looked at each other and then gazed down at the trail coming up the mountain. Dozens of people seemed to be heading our way.

As the rest of the group continued to talk to Joseph, discussing the Tenth with him, I walked farther out on the overhang, needing to think. I was still concerned by how quickly I had slipped into revenge.

How pervasive, I wondered, was this emotion in the world right now? Was it the predominating emotion behind the rash of school shootings, employee outbursts, and—on the international scene—the willingness to blow oneself and others up in order to make the enemy pay? Was this the way human fear and anger, in this time of transition, was playing out: wanting others to suffer the way we were suffering?

Colonel Peterson had said this Cycle of Revenge was growing into a nuclear phase, the urge to deliver the final act of retribution and end everything. I suddenly felt as if humanity was running out of time.

Where was Tommy? I wondered. I needed to speak with Tommy. When I turned around, I saw that he was already walking toward me. I laughed out loud, evoking a puzzled look from the young man.

"I need to talk to you," he said. "It's important."

"About the Universal Consciousness?" I asked.

"Yes, I want to tell you something. My tribe believes it will get much stronger, and sooner than most people think."

"But when is it going to happen?" I asked.

"Most think the Calendar's end date is December 21, 2012, but other scholars are saying the beginning of the last phase of creation will start much earlier, in the spring of 2011."

"What? That's now!"

"Yes. And we aren't going to understand this coming force of creation until we can figure out what the point of Connection we felt on Secret Mountain really is, and how to relate to it. We have to get through the remaining Integrations!"

Suddenly, Coleman was pushing his way through us to see down toward the guardhouse again.

"Look at that," he said with alarm.

Fifty or more troops were deploying all around the area of the guardhouse.

"They don't want any of those new people to come up the trails," Joseph said, "and I also think they know the extremists are around, and they want to stop them."

"The Apocalyptics are already past them," I stressed. "They're holed up near a mound of rock over the next ridge."

"How do you know that?" Coleman asked.

"I saw them when I was up there earlier with Rachel."

They all looked at me in amazement, and then Coleman said, "It's going to be difficult to sneak past all these troops."

"It's okay," I replied. "Rachel showed me another way past. It's almost dark. I think we should go now."

In a matter of minutes we were moving off the overhang and

down the slope. I remembered the route clearly. It would take us down the ridge to a point about a hundred yards to the right of the guardhouse. There, the trail ended at a steep drop-off into a wide gorge that seemed clearly impassable. What no one seemed to know, besides Rachel, was that a ledge wide enough for a person to walk on existed just over the edge of the gorge.

It ran a hundred feet north to a point where there was a small gap in the cliff wall that was scalable. Once through the gap we would be hidden from anyone looking from the guardhouse, and we could then advance directly up the tiers of rock overlooking the Apocalyptics to where Rachel and I had been earlier. The only place that was particularly close to the guardhouse was the point where we dropped down onto the ledge.

As we walked, I could see that Joseph had integrated the Ninth and Tenth steps, and now he, Coleman, and the others were reading the Eleventh. I thought of the old Prophecy and the Eleventh Insight that had grown out of it. It predicted the actualization of the use of intention and prayer, and learning the secrets of using this power.

"Do you believe what this Document is saying?" I suddenly heard Coleman shout.

I turned to see him talking to one of the scientists. Coleman shook has head in amazement and walked up to me, pointing at the Document.

"Listen how specific it is about the Influence," he said. " 'Because of the Law of Connection, the whole of what we believe and stand for—the quality of our character—sends out a field of Influence that impacts everyone with whom we interact. It acts to draw them into our level of consciousness and behavior, for good or ill, and either makes it easier or harder for them to stay in Alignment. And, at the same time, our individual Influence also co-mingles with everyone else's Influence globally, and at any one time helps to collectively set an energetic level of consciousness for all of humanity.' "

He was trying to stay beside me as we moved down the rugged terrain.

"Do you believe it?" he went on. "It's like there is a huge balance scale in the sky, weighing the relative strength of two opposing fields of Influence. One side represents those opening to a higher personal spirituality, and thus acting to lift others into that consciousness. The other side of the scale represents those who are still stuck in fear and anger, who are acting to pull people down into a simmering, untruthful fear and rage."

The statement hit me hard. That meant there was a contagion from both sides, and the balance shifted daily depending on how consistently those in Alignment could hold their truth with others.

"Do you see what this is?" Coleman added. "It's confirmation of Kant's categorical imperative: *Act and be as though how you are dictates that everyone else will be that same way.* His peers thought he was crazy. But his intuition was absolutely correct. Influence works exactly this way!"

I caught his eye. "Rachel said that we would integrate how to amplify our positive influence together. Does the Document say how?"

Coleman was looking intently at the pages in his hand. "It says the first thing we must do is keep the balance scale fully in mind at all times, and to remember that every thought and every action reverberates far beyond ourselves.

"It also says if enough of us fail to hold the energy of Alignment, the world could slip into even more fear and anger. In politics that would mean the far Left and Right will continue their dehumanization of the other until one side does something extreme, usually an act of despotism to take over and control, out of a need to save the world. In the area of religious ideology, the polarization goes more negative as well. It says that in prior cases in history, the antagonism has always gone as far as the current technology could take it."

We looked at each other, knowing that for this time period that meant an escalation to the nuclear level.

Suddenly, I realized we were nearing the guardhouse, where we had to be very careful. We could see individual soldiers patrolling in the area just below us, so I suggested to the others that they stay hidden while I moved back up the slope to take a better look.

As I climbed, I saw a movement above me and froze. As I strained to see who it was, the figure moved into plain view. It was one of Peterson's operatives, motioning for me to come up. When I arrived, he pulled me out of sight and whispered something into a microphone mounted near his mouth. In five minutes, Peterson was standing in front of me.

"What are you doing here?" he said. "We've been following your movements. And we can't make any sense of them."

"It's all intuitive," I said. "The Document says that in order to keep rising in Influence, we have to return to the Mount. Something's going to happen up there."

He shook his head skeptically. "What else is this Document saying about Influence?"

"We're finally understanding the power of intention and prayer. We're going to learn how to amplify our Influence."

"That's it?" he said. "All you have left is prayer?!"

"It's more than ordinary prayer," I protested. "You have to be seeking a higher level of experience. Otherwise, you may add to the energy of those Apocalyptics up there." I was looking at the next ridge ahead of us.

"Whoa!" he said, clearly shaken. "Are you telling me the Apocalyptics are up in these mountains somewhere?"

"Yeah, they're up ahead about five hundred yards. We think

someone in the Egyptian army is keeping the soldiers from going anywhere near them."

He looked away, thinking, then said, "This is another piece of the puzzle. We know they have something planned in Jerusalem and in Saudi Arabia on the mountain where there's a missile base. Now they're here. They're planning a whole chain of events that they think will bring the world to war. I told you, the charges are already placed under the Dome of the Rock."

I looked at him, puzzled.

"Don't you see?" he said. "They think they have to do everything according to scriptural Prophecy, which means Armageddon can't come until David's temple in Jerusalem is rebuilt. The Muslim mosque, the Dome of the Rock, is in the way. It has to be removed, so they're going to blow it up.

"The Judeo-Christian faction in the Apocalyptic group is pushing for this, because they already have the capstone from the original temple. They think if the capstone is quickly placed on the foundation, then it counts as if the rebuilding is underway. So the biblical Prophecy can be said to be fulfilled. After that, all they have to do is get the fighting started."

"But all those prophecies can happen in a different way!" I said, intuiting it fully now.

"Look," he replied, "we have to get real. We're right on the edge here. Do you hear me? We're right on the edge. Sooner or later this Apocalyptic plot is going to start, and it's going to create complete chaos in the Western countries.

"Iran already has missiles that can completely close the Suez Canal and the Strait of Hormuz. That's where most of the oil for the West originates. When this war gets started, gasoline will rise to thirty dollars a gallon. That alone could cause food shortages and hoarding. If China gets involved, there could be a simultaneous cyber attack on us. Then the lights could go out. What do you think would happen then? No gas, no food in the stores. Hundreds of thousands in the streets, rioting."

He paused and looked at me. "If anyone, us or otherwise, goes in and tries to stop these extremists piecemeal, the charges go off and the whole thing escalates. The wild card is Saudi Arabia. We don't know how that plays out exactly, because your government should be able to control whether those missiles are fired or not. And I don't know what they are planning here at Sinai, either, but you can bet it isn't good. That's why we're going forward with our plan to intervene. We can't wait. "

"No, listen," I said. "Your actions are as extreme as those of the Apocalyptics. You're planning to take over tyrannically because you think it's the only way to save Western culture!"

I could hear the others looking for me down below, calling my name.

"Listen," I said, "I have to go, but you must understand: the Document says if enough people get consciously involved in using their Influence, we can stop this war another way."

He was shaking his head. "It can't be stopped. It will erupt in the Middle East, and only if my group acts quickly can we counter the Chinese and contain the war. A lot of people will protest, but we can deal with that, too. And besides, you're not going anywhere. You're getting an escort out of here right now. You've had your chance."

He raised his radio to his lips.

"Wait a minute," I said. "You gave me five days, remember? That gives us through tomorrow."

I held the Agape, merging with his higher self. His expression softened ever so slightly, and he looked at me with a kind of longing, wishing the situation wasn't so bad.

After a long moment, he said, "Okay, you have one more day. We run the risk of you stumbling around up here and starting a war. But you know, I guess that's okay. We have everything in place to do what we have to do. We're ready."

"Come on," I whispered to the others when I got close. "Let's go." I grabbed my pack, my hands shaking slightly. The group followed me around a large outcropping and down toward the gorge.

Luckily, the soldiers were now running up to where Peterson was, so we took our opportunity to slip over the edge of the gorge, out of sight, and head up the ledge toward the Mount.

As we hurried up the slope, I moved closer to Coleman again and told him what Peterson had said. He shook his head and forced a smile. I could tell he was struggling to keep his energy up.

"What else is the Document saying?" I asked.

"It says the solution is the same for all time periods. In politics, an enlightened center, aligned in an open discussion of the truth, has to emerge to end the outright manipulation of voters and the corruption from both Left and Right.

"And in religion, an equally truthful group made up of the tolerant center of every religious tradition, all seeking the direct experience to which we have access, has to take center stage. No longer would one tradition try to impose their doctrine on other people or claim their way is the only path to Divine Connection. All religions would begin to emphasize those aspects of their traditions that are in line with this Connection, so that the religions would move closer to the truth and to one another."

Now he stopped dead in the pathway, looking down at the Document.

"This is important," he stressed. "It says the final part of the Eleventh Integration occurs when people in Alignment everywhere, across all cultures and religions, consciously begin to tune in to *each other*."

Of course, I thought. We have to tune in one more time at a higher level.

"How does it say to do that?" I asked.

"By consciously connecting in Agape not only with those we can make eye contact with but with everyone all around the world. We do that by intending and envisioning such a Connection fully in our minds. The Document says when this Connection is made, the natural influence of the individuals involved is amplified many times."

I nodded and concentrated on the climb, which was increasing in difficulty. After many hours of weaving in and out of crevices and jumping across small ravines—where we had to toss our backpacks to one another—we climbed onto the fortlike overlook where Rachel and I had been together earlier. The sun had long set, and a hazy dusk was descending over the mountain. We could see the bare outline of the rocky mound down below. Behind it, I knew, were the Apocalyptics.

I awakened the next day just before dawn, as usual, and got up quickly, knowing this would be an eventful day. Outside, I found everyone still asleep, which was not surprising. We had been up late talking about the Eleventh Integration.

Wil drifted into my mind. We hadn't heard from him since his last text, which said he would soon be on his way back to us. The question now was how would he find us. I pulled out the phone and checked. No texts from him. I wasn't surprised. He wouldn't risk using the phone to get directions.

Suddenly, I caught sight of the faint glow of flashlights far down the slope. I leaned over the rocks to watch the activity. Fortunately, the lights were heading away from us, so I relaxed again. Our climb had been much more difficult than I had remembered with Rachel, and I knew it would be equally difficult for anyone else to reach us now.

As I walked around, I suddenly realized Coleman was making noise on the other side of his tent. When he saw me, he handed me a cup of coffee. In the other hand was a pair of binoculars.

"It's about dawn," he said. "Want to see if we can spot the Apocalyptics?"

I nodded, and we walked over to the edge of the outcropping and hunkered down behind its natural raised edges. As I peered out through the early morning haze, I realized our position here was situated perfectly. From this vantage point, we could see not only the mound of rock where the extremists were hiding, but also the large, massive summit of Mount Sinai towering above us, and all the trails leading up to it.

The mound itself was about a hundred yards down the incline directly in front of us. For fifteen minutes we waited until it was light enough for Coleman to use his binoculars. The others awakened, one by one, and joined us.

"I see them," Coleman suddenly said. "They're doing something to the rock bed just beyond the mound."

Abruptly, I saw an image in my mind of myself going down to get a closer look. The image was accompanied by a surge of urgent energy. I grimaced at the idea and lowered my head. Tommy was behind me and noticed.

"What's wrong?" he asked.

"I think I need to go down there and take a look. Anybody else get that idea?"

No one responded.

"Are you sure you want to do that?" Coleman asked. "Remember the Second Integration: logic first."

"I know it's dangerous, but too much has happened for me not to follow an intuition now. Rachel followed all of hers."

For a moment, the whole group looked at me, and I could see the determination building.

"I better go with you," Coleman said finally.

I tuned in to whether I was down there alone or with someone, and could see only myself.

"Looks like I have to go it alone this time."

Turning to Tommy and his mother, I asked them for advice on the route and they pointed out the way they would go, giving me encouragement.

"We'll focus on helping you," Tommy said, "like the Angels."

I gave him a pat on the shoulder and eased down over the ledge as the sun broke above the horizon for the first time. Focusing on the beauty, I managed to hold my energy as I crept down the rocky slope. I thought about my father's advice on how to keep one's wits while in situations of extreme danger. And smiled. I knew he was around.

At last, I arrived at a spire of rock that rose up about twenty-five feet in front of me. Very carefully, I crawled forward and gazed over. Within fifty feet of me, about a dozen men were covering something in a twelve-foot crevice with rocks. Anish was nowhere to be seen.

Then I spotted someone sitting alone, his hands tied behind his back. He turned his head, and my stomach seized. It was Wil!

I stared at him until he felt me looking and jerked around and saw me. He immediately began to point with his eyes toward the ground to his left, where a handheld two-way radio was sitting on an old leather briefcase on the ground. I was bewildered. What did he want me to do? Grab the radio? I couldn't understand how that would help us.

Suddenly, I heard a noise in the rocks directly below me. I rolled backward quietly and dropped into a mild depression in the rock, hoping to hide. The noise continued, and to my horror I realized someone was climbing the same spire I was lying on, coming my way. I tried to duck down but it was too late. The individual, holding a pair of binoculars, had climbed to a point just ten feet below me. Anish.

He turned and looked, recognizing me immediately.

"I thought you were around here somewhere," he said. "I could feel you. You're like me. You never give up."

His tone and demeanor were casual, even serene, again like someone feeling invulnerable. Rachel had tried to reach him, and now it was my turn. As best I could, I tried to center myself and move into Oneness, hoping he might sense his own Divine Connection.

"I have to talk to you," I said. "I don't know what you're doing, but you have to rethink it. There's another way."

"Will you stop exporting your corruption to my world? Will you stop trying to reform my religion?"

I sat up so he could see me better. "We all have souls. We're all the same, spiritually. It's true, there's too much corruption everywhere. But we can fix that, all of us together, if we find the one experience."

He laughed and gave me a look of pity. "The prophets don't lie! The end must come now."

For a moment there was only silence. I didn't know what to say. Then I thought of Rachel and remembered my last conversation with her.

"The Prophecies all point to an Armageddon," I stressed. "And a Rapture where the true believers are protected, so they can avoid this war. What if the message of the prophets is really for all of us? And the message is that we can all find a higher God Connection together that will allow us to avoid Armageddon? Do you see what I'm saying? Armageddon doesn't have to happen!"

I could feel Rachel wanting me to say something else about the Calendar and about the point of Connection I had felt on Secret Mountain, but I couldn't put it together in my mind.

Anish looked at me, first in confusion and then in anger. When he reached inside his belt for a weapon, I was ready. I rolled over and slipped off the crest of the huge rock on the side away from him. As I did, I glimpsed from the corner of my eye the item the extremists were covering up. It was about the size of a suitcase and had several blinking lights on one side.

For a minute or two, I ran up the hill frantically, thinking he was chasing me. Then I heard him yell from back at the mound.

"If I see you again," he called out, "your friend will be the first to die."

When I got back to the others, I was so out of breath and exhausted from the climb that I couldn't tell them anything for a full minute.

"They have Wil!" I finally blurted out. "I tried to convince Anish to stop what he was doing, but it didn't work. There wasn't enough energy. They have some kind of device."

Coleman was listening intensely. "What did the device look like?"

"It's a boxlike item," I said, "like a small suitcase with handles. There are lights on one side."

He grimaced and stared at all of us. Our hearts sank. We knew what he was going to say.

"It has to be a small nuke," he voiced.

We were all shocked and speechless. Everyone's fear had just turned into a reality.

"Why here?" Tommy finally asked.

"Probably," I guessed, "to make it look as if someone had attacked Egypt, so that other countries would retaliate, igniting the war."

For a long moment, we were all alone with our thoughts, knowing this could be the end. Every one of us might die right here on Mount Sinai.

Then I saw something down below. Hundreds of people were approaching Mount Sinai from all directions, pressing up against the checkpoints and being held back at gunpoint by the soldiers.

"Hurry," Tommy shouted. "We have to connect with them."

THE RETURN

Tommy was gathering us all together at the top of the outcropping. Down below, the crowds were becoming larger every minute.

"First," Tommy was saying, the Document in his lap, "we have to amplify Agape with one another and with the Great Spirit."

We all elevated into that Connection in seconds.

"Then," he continued, "it says to project the Agape to ever larger groups, by intending Oneness with everyone who is genuinely seeking spiritual Connection, across all religions, especially those down below us."

As we did so, our energy increased even more until we regained the level of collective intention that we had felt spontaneously on Secret Mountain. For a moment we looked at one another, feeling the Eleventh elevation fully, then immediately went into a template discussion.

Joseph quickly pointed out that while most traditions emphasized prayer, some, like the Sufi of Islam, advocated a lived prayer very close to what we were feeling now.

"Christianity," I said quickly, "also strongly emphasizes the power of collective prayer." In minutes, we agreed that the emphasis placed on prayer by Islam and Christianity most reflected the reality of connected group intention. A rush of energy from the agreement sent us soaring even higher.

I looked at my phone, knowing what was about to occur. The text ring sounded twice, and I opened it to find messages from Hira and Adjar, both expressing heartbreak about Rachel and telling us they had worked through the Tenth and Eleventh Integrations and were feeling Unity with us and her. They were making preparations to reach out more widely, mentioning that hundreds of people were collecting in Jerusalem and near the Mount in Saudi Arabia.

For several long minutes, we focused on the people down below, and those in Jerusalem and Saudi Arabia. At first nothing happened, and then slowly we began to see individuals at the checkpoints grouping together as though they were picking up on what we were doing. Some had copies of the Document and were showing them to others. People near the soldiers began to reach out and talk to them as well.

"Bring the soldiers into Agape with us," Tommy said. "See them lifting up into their own Connection with Spirit."

Almost instantly, we could see some of the soldiers lowering their weapons. Some even joined the group that seemed to be forming. Looking angry, the officers came forward and tried to stop the interaction, but some soldiers were allowing individuals to walk past them and head up the trails toward the summit.

At the mound, we could see the Apocalyptics looking over the rocks at the scene below. Anish glared up directly at us, obviously concerned.

"Look at that," I said to Coleman. "He knows what we're doing."

"Focus on the Apocalyptics!" Tommy yelled.

I pictured seeing a higher expression on their faces that reflected their souls' desire to move into Connection. After a while, several of the extremists actually left their positions to see what the crowd was doing.

Suddenly, my phone rang twice. It was Hira and Adjar, telling us the crowds there were pushing forward at both the Temple Mount and the Saudi Mount, Jabal Al Lawz.

Then Coleman shouted, "Look over at the mound!"

Anish was out among his group, shouting and gesturing dramatically with his arms. The men hurriedly began picking up their guns and strengthening their positions. From behind him, another man walked up hesitantly behind Anish. It was the round military general we had seen earlier.

"That's my brother," Joseph shouted. "I've been focusing on him. Help me!" Joseph took off over the edge of the outcropping and ran down the slope toward the mound.

Before I could react, I heard a gasp from Tommy's mother. She was looking in the direction of the crowds down below again. More troops had arrived and were pushing people back down the slope. Several began firing their automatic weapons into the air. With each burst, I could feel our energy waning.

Again my phone rang with a text, and I looked at it quickly. It was Adjar saying that more soldiers had arrived there as well and were pushing everyone back. Seconds later, another text rang. It was Hira saying the same thing was happening in Jerusalem.

I looked back at the crowds and saw they were being pushed back even farther. Barricades were being set up. We were failing.

"Hold your energy," I shouted, trying to focus.

Coleman grabbed my shoulders. "We aren't strong enough! We haven't yet regained the full consciousness we had on Secret Mountain! We need the Twelfth!"

Immediately, I thought about the point of Connection we'd experienced on Secret Mountain, and in a flash I seemed to feel it again. I looked at Coleman and his expression told me he was feeling the same thing. Tommy, obviously sensing it, too, rushed over.

"This is the Connection we had," he yelled. "We have to hold this, build on it."

As soon as Tommy made that statement, we couldn't feel the point of Connection anymore. It had completely disappeared.

"What happened?" Tommy asked.

I was struggling to remember my earlier experience.

"Wait," I stressed. "You can't force it. You have to allow it or have faith in it or something."

As soon as I spoke those words, we could feel it again, but it was still sporadic, appearing for a moment and then disappearing.

"There's something we're missing!" I yelled. "What is it?"

Then I remembered. At the height of the Connection on Secret Mountain we had experienced another emotion I had forgotten about: a soulful sense of appreciation.

I also remembered something I had thought at the time. Appreciation was the act of acknowledgment that locked in the Connection. Immediately, I felt the Connection more intensely, and as I did, the Agape began to increase in slow increments, almost to the level we had achieved on Secret Mountain but not quite. Tommy and Coleman had already sensed what I was doing and were gathering the others back into a circle with us, explaining how to hold the emotion of appreciation.

Then I knew something more. We were calling this phenomenon a point of Connection, but in actuality it was something else. Rachel had said not to get hung up on a name. We had to understand more about what we were feeling. I no sooner had that thought when an image of Wil down there with the Apocalyptics came to mind. And then another image came—one of the radio sitting on the briefcase. In a flash I understood. Wil hadn't been nodding toward the radio, as I'd thought earlier. It was the briefcase he wanted me to see!

Down at the trails below, the shooting had stopped and the

soldiers and the crowds were now in an uneasy stalemate, the people still pressing to go forward, the soldiers holding fast.

"I've got to go back down there," I said to the others.

They voiced agreement, so without saying another word, I slid off the outcropping again and hurried down the slope, trying to hang on to the Connection. The others were right behind me. Coleman caught up with me and smiled as we jumped a wide crevice in the rock. When we approached the mound, we could see two men wrestling over a rifle and several more fighting twenty feet away. We avoided them and ran around to the side of the rocky protrusion. Now we could see Anish and some of his own men in an armed standoff. Some of the men had awakened and were now pointing weapons and begging for Anish to give up. Joseph and his brother were in that group. Anish and several other men were facing them, unyielding, still in control of the bomb. One of the men held a small remote control in his hand, apparently the triggering device for the nuke.

Closer to us, Wil was still sitting in the same place. But he had managed to free his feet and hands in the confusion, and at his side was the briefcase, now open. Four or five pages of copy paper were scattered beside it. Our eyes met, and I instantly knew the pages belonged to the Twelfth, and that he had already read it. I noticed, too, that my hands were shaking again. I had lost much of my Connection in the face of the conflict. Still locked in Wil's stare, I went deep into Agape until I began to feel the point of Connection again.

Right away, I realized Wil was trying to tell me something again, but I couldn't hear him amid the shouting.

"Be prepared to detonate," Anish said, gathering everyone's attention. He seemed to have regained his calm determination.

I looked at Wil. He was still looking at me intently, sending me a message with his eyes. Behind me were Coleman, Tommy, and his mother. The rest of the group were several paces behind them.

Down below, I could see the crowds still pressing against the soldiers' barricades.

Anish squinted with final resolve, about to order detonation. I looked at Wil one more time, and finally got it. Rachel. He wanted me to tune in to Rachel. Immediately, I felt her saying, "Let go! You'll be shown the way."

"Wait a m-minute!" I stammered at Anish. "Can't you feel what's happening here? You had the Twelfth Integration the whole time. You must have read it!"

Anish shook his head. "The only thing I feel is the end of time approaching."

"But that's just it! Something is approaching, but it's not what you think. It's something you have to feel inside."

Anish looked at me askance.

"Ask yourself," I continued, "why you formed this group in the first place, including both Eastern and Western traditions. The members were all mortal enemies and you brought them together. Was it the Twelfth Insight that gave you that idea? You began a reconciliation of religion. And you continued to look for more of the Document for a long time. Why? Maybe you knew you weren't going far enough."

He looked away, shaking his head.

"Why did you name your group the Apocalyptics?" I continued. "Don't you know the word *apocalypse* means revelation? We can have a revelation about the real meaning of the end times. I tried to tell you. The prophecies are meant for all of us. If all of us are engaged in one Rapture, then we can all be spared Armageddon. We get the Return without the war. We're already sensing..."

I stopped. I still couldn't explain this point of Connection we were feeling.

"No," Anish screamed, looking again at the man with the detonator. Again he appeared to be ready to order the detonation.

Someone to his right yelled, "You must stop!"

Joseph's brother, the general, was walking up to Anish now, Joseph at his side.

"You know you and I both read those words," the general continued. "We laughed and ridiculed it at every page, but it was touching us all the same."

Anish became enraged and pointed a finger at the general. "What has happened to you?" he screamed. "You know our plan is foolproof. A nuclear blast here in Sinai and the simultaneous destruction of the Dome of the Rock in Jerusalem will push Iran to blow the canal. Saudi Arabian missiles, under our control, will fly at Iran. Our people in China will take the opportunity to disable the American capability in that region. And then everything will blow! Nothing could contain it, not even Peterson. It would be the end we've all been praying for."

"No," Joseph's brother said firmly. "The prophecies are all saying the same thing because they come from only one Divine source. I know that now! There's only one Creator, and only one Rapture: the one that comes from attaining an ever-higher Connection and consciousness. We are already sensing the Divine return. It is a 'Presence' that we can feel within us."

"That's it!" I yelled. "That's what we're feeling. It's a Divine Presence!"

The sound of the words reverberated through everyone. Will and I looked at each other. That is what we had felt on Secret Mountain: the Presence of God as a tangible reality. This was the return the prophecies had been pointing toward all along, the final Alignment.

Thoughts raced through my mind over the magnitude of what was happening. It was not the idea of a presence, nor an abstract theory about a presence. It was an *actual* Presence: the Feeling Identity of the Divine—real and personal and with us at this very moment.

With that thought, my energy and consciousness began to soar, and I could detect the Presence increasing inside me. Time stood still. The Apocalyptics appeared frozen. I looked over at Wil again. He was nodding in excitement. Coleman was sending a text to Adjar and Hira telling them what we had discovered. Tommy and the others were awestruck.

As we glanced at one another, the energy increased more. We were recapturing together that final level of energy we had glimpsed in the wilderness of Sedona. Instantly, I sensed what the rest of the group was thinking. This was it: the Twelfth Insight and its Integration. We can open our consciousness enough to reach the actual Presence of the Divine, right here where it has always been waiting for us.

Spontaneously, we all fell into a Template of Agreement. I could feel our conclusion. All of the traditions hold that God is a real presence, but it has only been emphasized and really thought possible in the most esoteric religious teachings.

"Acknowledge the Presence in appreciation and the link will get stronger," I heard Tommy whisper to the others. "This will connect our final template conclusion with all those in the world who are sensing this."

No sooner had we done this than our energy soared even more.

"Now join with the higher souls of the Apocalyptics," Tommy added, "and lift them into this new Connection with us."

As we did so, the presence increased to another level, and its character changed. Now it was not only inside of us, it was also outside as well, manifesting as a perceptible wave of luminosity all around the mound area. Then it swept down toward the crowds in a wave that lit up the rocks as it went.

Down at the trails, we could see people reaching out to the soldiers again, pushing at the barricade lines, darting around the weapons aimed at them, and moving all at once, as though of one mind, up the trails.

Then, in a scene reminiscent of the fall of the old Soviet Union, the soldiers broke ranks and refused to fire, throwing down their weapons. Commanders stopped shouting orders, resigned to the inevitable. Some soldiers were actually joining the flow of people toward the summit.

Anish turned and looked at me, and for a moment I thought he was going to get it. Then his face hardened again.

"Blow the bomb!" he screamed.

"No," I yelled. "Don't you understand? It's okay to reverse your life direction. You don't have to push that button. You can change."

The man with the detonator was hesitating, listening to me, not moving. So Anish suddenly charged him, grabbing at the device. It fell to the rocks. He hurled himself toward it, stretching out his arms to pick it up. But Joseph's brother rushed up to block his grasp.

Then gunshots began to ring out as the two factions exchanged fire. Reacting swiftly, Joseph ran toward his brother and knocked him behind a boulder. Simultaneously, Wil lunged forward and hit me in full stride, also pushing me out of harm's way. A single grenade exploded, covering us with smoke and dust.

When I could see, I realized most of the Apocalyptics had fled. Wil and Coleman were sitting beside me. We all just looked at one another, knowing how fortunate we had been that the bomb hadn't detonated. Looking around, we saw that Anish and another extremist were seriously wounded and Joseph's brother had superficial cuts. No one else was hurt. Above us, hundreds were on the summit of Mount Sinai, waving their hands in celebration.

In minutes, we were surrounded by fresh Egyptian soldiers, a whole battalion of them, who provided immediate medical care and order. Hundreds more soldiers were quickly moving up the trails, ushering the crowds off the summit. The people didn't resist, realizing clearly that the day had been won. Our group was rejoicing as well. At least for now, the threat was over.

One of the officers, a lieutenant, took our group into custody and sat us down by the mound, taking particular interest in Tommy and Joseph and pulling them to the side. He was the officer Tommy had been talking with for months at the eastern gate. The three discussed the situation intensely for several minutes, gesturing toward the rest of us.

Just then my phone rang. It was Adjar, updating us on the situation at Jabal Al Lawz, saying that the template groups had gained the Twelfth Insight and Integration simultaneously with us. The infiltrators from within the missile base had fled. Right after Adjar, Hira also texted, on cue. They had not reached the Temple Mount but instead had gathered at the Wailing Wall at the moment of reaching the Twelfth. No confirmation, she said, about the rumored charges under the Dome of the Rock.

Finally, I heard the officer say, "Get them out of here!"

Joseph and Tommy rushed over and pointed out the path leading back to St. Katherine, telling us we were free to leave. We all just looked at one another and erupted in laughter.

Suddenly, I noticed some papers blowing along the ground back near the mound. Rushing over, I was just about to reach down and pick them up when another man, whom I recognized as one of Peterson's operatives, stepped in front of me and scooped them up himself, giving me a half smile and a small shake of his head.

All around me, I could see people being thoroughly searched, and anything remotely looking like a copy of the Integrations was seized. When they reached us, we didn't resist.

I wondered: did Peterson now think the Document was a threat to him? Was he moving to find and destroy all the copies, the same way the government of Peru had managed to destroy all the copies of the old Prophecy? At best, I reasoned, he could create enough fear so that people would feel guarded about talking about the Document and would keep their copies hidden. Such a suppression, I knew, would have to include an immediate cleansing of the Internet of all traces.

When I got back to the others, Joseph was saying good-bye, telling us he would stay there with his wounded brother.

"Thanks," I said, "for being on that hill in St. Katherine when we arrived."

He gave me a smile and a little bow of his head.

"Also," Wil added, "thanks for not giving up on your brother. Whatever you said to him worked. Just shows us: reach one person and it may make all the difference in the world."

"I simply told him," Joseph responded, "what Rachel had said to me: anyone can wake up and change in the blink of an eye."

"Oh, by the way," Joseph went on, "did I tell you the three Mountains—Jabal Al Lawz in Saudi Arabia, Mount Sinai, and Secret Mountain in Arizona—all line up roughly in a straight line?"

He looked at us a moment more with his face filling with Agape and tears, then he pulled us into a huge hug.

"I wanted to look upon the face of God," he mused, "but I think feeling the Presence is even better."

As he walked away, the rest of us, lost in our own thoughts, hiked down the mountain until we hit the wide path taking us back to St. Katherine. Wil was on his phone. As I looked around at everyone, I could tell we were all still feeling the Presence. It was with us as we moved down the path, automatically raising the luminosity of the rocks as we walked. When we met people coming toward us, some would even slow down and look closely, as if they sensed the elevation in energy.

When Wil hung up his phone, I edged over beside him.

"Okay, Wil," I said, "what about the Twelfth? Tell us what the Document actually says."

His eyes twinkled for a moment as everyone gathered around him.

"It says the Twelfth fires up the culminating pathways in our brains," he said. "It integrates all the Integrations. Think about how the Presence makes you feel. No problem with expecting and sustaining the Synchronicity now, is there? Or telling the truth and accepting it from others as we build out the details of our new spiritual worldview? How about manipulating people and being hit with all that Karma? Anybody want to start doing that again?

"No," he continued. "We want to stay in Alignment and in the consciousness that gives us all these other abilities: premonitions that offer us Protection, guiding intuition, higher Agape relationships, and an opening to full perception—and of course, all those messages from the Afterlife.

"The Twelfth says that if enough of us stay in this Alignment and in the Presence, the Plan can become conscious in human culture. With this knowledge, an enlightened center way will arise in politics. Civility and charm can return to human culture. And every government and every field of human endeavor will move into a state of Integrity."

"What about the Templates of Agreement?" Coleman asked.

"It says the Templates of Agreement will gradually move each tradition," Wil replied, "toward an acknowledgment of the one Presence, allowing the differences between the religions to be less divisive. Reconciliation will create a groundbreaking unity as we all focus on the experience that is possible." He paused. "The numbers are everything. It just depends on how many people are holding the Alignment."

As he talked, a question was forming in my mind.

"Does the Twelfth say," I asked, "how many people it would

take to turn the world around and to begin to create the ideal world the prophecies predict?"

"A lot, just to get it started. The Document mentions again that many smaller groups in history have reached the point where we are now and weren't able to keep it going. The world is still deep in fear. And as we've seen, the stakes are getting higher."

All of us were huddled just off the path, in a circle.

"Does the Twelfth give us the specific number?" I pressed.

"Yes," Wil said. "It is the same as with some of the other prophecies."

"What is it?"

"144,000."

As soon as we reached St. Katherine, Tommy and his mother said good-bye as well, stating that they wanted to visit their friends at the big house one more time. They had given everyone a hug and were beginning to walk away. But after only a few paces, Tommy stopped and turned toward me.

"There's much to be done," he added, "so I'll see you in Sedona."

He smiled then and ran to join his mother, leaving me wondering what he meant.

Most of the others said good-bye as well and went with them, leaving only Wil, Coleman, and me standing together on the street. Coleman offered his hand.

"I'm going with them, too," he said. "Some of my scientist friends want to start an institute to study all this. Do you believe it?"

He walked over and gave Wil and me both a bear hug.

"Listen," I said. "Thanks for being there all those times."

"I should thank you," he replied. "You reached me. It just shows how things change, one Conscious Conversation at a time."

Wil and I waved as he jogged off after the others, then Wil turned to face me.

"I was able to book a flight to Cairo," he said, smiling.

He then told me he had finally reached his friend the archaeologist, who had originally sent him the first part of the Document. The man had been in hiding, and Wil wanted to leave right away to talk to him.

He paused and we continued to look at each other, delaying the parting.

"What about Colonel Peterson?" Wil asked.

"The last thing he told me," I replied, "was that they were ready, and that all it takes is a coalition between the far Left and Right to implement his plan. I still don't know what he meant."

"I think you're going to find out," Wil said. "Better stay alert."

I nodded, then said, "I forgot to ask. Did you have any luck finding the people who had released this Document originally?"

He smiled and said, "You already know who it was."

I thought for a moment.

"Shambhala people?"

"There are more of them than I thought. They're going to be helping with everything. I'll let you know what I find out."

He was beginning to leave, but I thought of one last question.

"Why did they send the Twelfth to Anish?"

Wil laughed and pulled his pack onto his shoulder.

"They're like Wolf," he said. "They know things."

And with that, he was gone, leaving me alone. Only I wasn't alone. In fact, I knew I would never be alone again.

EPILOGUE

The next day, I booked flights through Cairo myself. But I didn't go back to Georgia. Instead, I went to Sedona. During the journey, the Presence was always there, and it didn't fade at all unless I fell into ego or became distracted in some way.

When that occurred, I had only to come back into Alignment again, and move into appreciation—and immediately the Presence was back. If nothing else, this consciousness was eminently provable to oneself.

With the Presence came the Agape and a kind of automatic expectation of Synchronicity and a remembering to make sure along the way that I had told the absolute truth to others—voicing especially the intuitive ideas that I felt they needed to hear. What made the most difference was the intention to merge higher minds with people. When I did that, the most ordinary of conversations would suddenly turn magical, and I would always receive something back.

After a while, I was able to experience what Wil had called "the integration of the integrations" just by being aware that this enveloping Presence came with me into an airplane, or a room full of people, often to the distinct perception of others. This recognition of sharing the Presence kept me in Alignment at an even higher level, and I knew that if enough of us were doing this, then the consciousness could quickly spread.

I found that the emerging Twelfth Insight was in no way just a theory. It was a new level of being that could be discovered and lived by any person, across all cultures and religions. If we keep the Presence with us and stay alert, the means necessary to be of service—and to make the world a better place—would always be provided.

The only real difficulty for any of us, I knew, in holding this consciousness, was the insidious effect of the old, material worldview. It is still out there, whispering in our ear, telling us the world is hard and unforgiving and that leading a life of some esoteric, saintly intent is impossible. That is true, of course, if we think of ourselves as being alone in a meaningless Universe. But the fact is, we aren't. We can stay in Alignment, and prove to ourselves that we live in a Universe that is, in essence, a Dream Machine—just waiting for us to turn it on.

Two days later, when I arrived in Sedona, I went immediately to the Airport Vortex and climbed up on the rocks to watch the sunset. There were only one or two other people there, so I took a seat on the very top and closed my eyes, feeling the warmth of the sinking sun on my face.

Suddenly someone sat down beside me with a plop. I looked around to see Tommy's smiling face.

"You came to tell me," I said, "that it's all going to be okay, didn't you?"

He gave me that look that made him seem so much older.

"I came to tell you that the flame of this consciousness must not be allowed to go out. This historical moment is too important. It is the hour of decision, and every person alive must make a choice."

He then looked at me as though he might burst out laughing. "After all, Dr. Coleman's scale is still up there in the sky, and every thought counts."

I nodded, then asked, "Tommy, have you received your tribal name yet?"

"Yes—last night, from the elders."

"What is it?"

"Mountain Timekeeper."

I smiled, knowing it was perfect. He would do his part to make the vision of the Calendar known.

We fell into silence then, and I gazed out at a familiar-looking sunset—little angel swirls of pink clouds, stark against a deep blue sky.

As I watched, my thoughts drifted again to the state of the world. Would, indeed, enough of us move into Alignment to meet the challenge? As I pondered the question, I heard a crow caw in the distance. And in that moment, I caught the faintest fragrance of rose in the air. Yes, I thought, I'm betting yes.

If you sense the truth of what is occurring and believe that people of integrity can make a difference, take action. To let us know what you are doing or to receive the latest commentaries by James Redfield, visit celestinevision.com.